a woman under a roof and other stories from the Chinese

David Hughes

A Woman Under a Roof and Other Stories from the Chinese
Copyright © 2012 by David Hughes
All Rights Reserved

ISBN: 978-0-9854414-0-1

Printed in the United States of America by
Gorham Printing
3718 Mahoney Drive
Centralia, WA 98531
http://www.gorhamprinting.com

To order additional copies, contact davidforser@me.com

Truth   and   Beauty

do not begin .... or end

at a

Political or Geographic

Boundary

Sherre —
I hope you enjoy
these stories.

David Hughes
August 2013

About the Author

David Hughes spent several decades as a diplomat with the Department of State and the Department of Commerce, as a university professor, and as an international businessman. With more than twenty-five years abroad, he has lived in nine different countries, including a decade in China, Hong Kong, and Taiwan. The 43 stories in this book reflect some of those experiences. He speaks Cantonese and Mandarin among other languages. His wife is from Taiwan.

Also by the author:

More Stories From Over There

and soon to be released:

Stories Not To Be Told.

These stories are intended to be read separately.

Thanks are due to family members, Foreign Service people, friends and neighbors, Richard Hugo House in Seattle and classmates in Nancy Kress' writing critique class, and to students of Carol Orlock, the author and professor who guided me through a writing class at the Women's University Club. The cover design is by Maria Hughes and Curtis Jackson. Thanks too to Lincoln Potter for the two great photos.

The Department of State has asked me to include the following, in accordance with an agreement I signed years ago: "The opinions and characterizations in these stories are those of the author, and do not necessarily represent the official positions of the United States Government."

Stories from the Chinese

Civilized	1
The Wife of the Political Prisoner	3
Culture Shock	9
Wiggly Things	15
The Incident in Guilin	17
The Nose	19
Yaht Yih Saam	23
They All Look the Same	25
Watch Your Dog, Marines	27
Grace and the Garbage Can	29
Cry for Me, Hong Kong	33
The Chinese Ambassador Solves the Balance of Payments Problem	39
Repudiated. Twice.	43

The May-run Stories

    An Arranged Marriage: Old Style 51

    An Arranged Marriage: New Style 61

    Dear May-run: 67

    Dear Wu-fen: 71

The Motorcycle Rider's Revenge 79

The Incident in New Bamboo 81

Poetic Justice 85

The Dance Hall Girl 89

A Woman Under a Roof 95

The Theft of an Artist 99

Three Kisses – Love 109

Three Kisses -- Humanity 117

Three Kisses -- Life 123

Paragraph 127

The Guangzhou Stories

The Top of the Fang Starring Kirk Douglas on the New Microwave	131
Bluebeard and the Vice President	135
Hunan	141
Take One for the Team – Chinese Style	143
Big Mac Comes to China	147
Frogs, Aristophanes, Frogs	153
Good News! Fragrant Meat	155
The Toilet Paper Caper	157
The Kangaroo Kaper	161
The Mystery of the Disappearing Business Card	165
Crouching Governor, Flying Tiger	169
The Great Chinese Bicycle Race	173
It's Cold South of the Yangzi River	177
The Handy Official	179
How We Stopped the Suicide of the Consul	183
Paragraphs	189

Stories from the Chinese

Civilized

The American Ambassador had been invited to give a speech to the Rotary Club of Taipei.

The Rotarians were very pleased to have such a distinguished visitor address them on a topic of his own choosing. It was known that the Ambassador did not speak Chinese, or at least not at the level where he could deliver a luncheon address in that language.

Though there was considerable competition among leading Rotarians to sit at the head table, it was readily agreed that preference would be given to those members who also spoke English so that the Ambassador could have an amiable and open conversation in the interval before his remarks.

Ambassadors, like many other public speakers, are aware of the need to lighten up their comments with occasional humorous stories, and the American Ambassador to the Republic of China was no exception to this general rule.

Not all of the Rotarians spoke English. While some spoke poorly, there were some Rotarians who did not speak any English at all.

The Ambassador's remarks would have to be translated, orally, by a Rotarian adept in both languages

When the lunch portion came to an end, the Club President arose and introduced the Ambassador.

The Ambassador arose in turn, began his remarks and then paused at suitable intervals for the remarks to be translated into Mandarin Chinese.

The Ambassador looked up in surprise when at his first humorous remark, in English, no one, not even the well-known English speakers, laughed, or even smiled. The Ambassador was, if anything, a well-practiced diplomat, and he decided to take no notice of the unresponsive audience.

As his remarks were translated into Chinese, there would be wide spread laughter at certain junctures. Initially, the Ambassador did not understand what was happening. Then it dawned upon him that out of a sense of consideration for the Rotarians who did not understand English, the English-speakers did not react to his remarks until they were put into Chinese. Thus there was no call for embarrassment or loss of face among colleagues who did not speak English. Under these circumstances, all of the Rotarians could laugh or nod assent at the same time.

Later on, the Ambassador was heard to mention to his staff that it was the most magnificent example of civilized behavior that had ever come to his attention.

The Wife of the Political Prisoner

She was a nice person. Maybe that had something to do with it.

Her husband had been arrested, and sent off who knows where. Probably to the political prison on Green Island where, unbeknownst to outsiders, the standard sentence was fifteen years. In any event, he was gone, locked up at least, rather than put on a small rickety rowboat, without oars, in the middle of the Taiwan Straits. She could infer that he was still alive.

She was a nice person. Married for life. She would not disown him.

They were Chinese, not Taiwanese, and had fled to Taiwan in the mad rush of 1949 as the communists took control of China. They came from an educated family that had never been enamored of the communists though they were chagrined that the only alternative was nearly as unpalatable. A Hobson's Choice was the way her husband had put it.

For a Beijing family, which had long disavowed ethnic animosities, they were surprised at the divisive nature of the relationship between the Chinese from mainland China and the local people, the Taiwanese. The husband and wife had felt quite uncomfortable with being *ipso facto* identified with the authoritarian regime solely because of their ethnicity. At home, they had gotten on well with Cantonese and their singsong pronunciation, and laughed over the witticism "I am not afraid of Heaven; I am not afraid of Hell; I am just afraid of Cantonese trying to speak Mandarin well." Similarly with Shanghai or Manchu friends. Her husband had said that he truly liked the variations of Chinese spoken by the different peoples of China. It was enriching, stimulating, exciting, and kept your ear, and mind, sharp. While many Beijing citizens were convinced that the only proper Chinese was that spoken in Beijing, neither of them followed such a narrow dictum. No Harvard accent for them, if you please.

Her husband liked to talk, which had evidently gotten him in trouble. When he was arrested, taken away, she was nevertheless shocked. He was hardly the revolutionary. Her own interrogation by the security services was short, shortened perhaps by the threats to her welfare made to her husband who understood the significance of those threats. If he cooperated, she would not be harmed. Being "harmed" by the security services in an authoritarian regime was not a pleasant fate to contemplate, especially for a woman. He had evidently cooperated; laying on himself thoughts and ideas that could not have been true.

She often asked herself, "How can I tell him that I love him under these circumstances? Where are the ears to hear the words?

Where is the smile to acknowledge the expression, this voicing of three words that mean so much?"

Though emotionally devastated, she still had to assert that streak of practicality that runs through so many people in adversity. She had to deal with the reality thrust upon her. She had to live, no matter how bereft she felt. She had to be there when he came home.

In Taiwan, Chinese often felt trapped, trapped by being Chinese in a polarized ethnic environment. Maybe guilty is a better word. Guilty of being Chinese. How could one be a human if those around you were obliged by circumstance to view one as a Chinese?

Ethnic divides can, however, have some left-handed benefits. It was a widely held opinion throughout Taiwan that Chinese companies hired Chinese, Taiwanese companies hired Taiwanese. Knowing that she would have to earn her living alone, she thought to apply for a job with China Airlines (CAL), a company whose employees were almost entirely Chinese. She could complete the application form easily enough. Her birthplace and her education virtually guaranteed her a job. She was hired almost immediately. No other questions.

She worked at CAL, making a progressively good impression on her workmates until one day, six months after she had started, her supervisor came to her in tears, saying, 'We have been advised by the authorities that your husband is in prison. We can't employ someone with such a background." The wife of the political prisoner left that day, stunned at the meanness of the authorities.

She got another job, in a mostly Chinese insurance company. It was enough to keep body, if not soul, together. One day, some months later, as she was walking through the market, she ran into her former supervisor at China Airlines. The woman who had cried when discharging her months earlier told the prisoner's wife that there were new openings at the airline. Perhaps she could apply. She did, and was hired on the spot. She worked hard during this second stint at China Airlines trying to make herself valuable. She succeeded quite well, was liked by her colleagues, and did whatever was asked, and perhaps a little bit more.

Once again, however, the dreaded visit by the security services resulted in her supervisor informing her that she was fired effective immediately. Six months appeared to be her allowable tenure before pressure by the security services resulted in her unceremonious termination.

Again, she sought out what she knew would be temporary employment, secured a job, and once more, after several months, was terminated without ceremony. And yet she thought, perhaps she could go back to China Airlines.

She did, and was hired, a third time. Surely, she thought, the employment office at CAL would know of her association. And in fact, they did. They understood that after a few months, the security services would come by and "urge" her to be fired. Still CAL hired her, ready to explain to the authorities that they didn't know it was the same woman, or that they hadn't checked previous employment records, or that the person hiring her had inadvertently overlooked the information on file.

The periodic hiring and subsequent firing went on for several years. *Déjà vu* all over again, and again, for the wife of the political prisoner.

Yet why did CAL continue to hire and re-hire the wife of the political prisoner?

Could it be that others who had been caught up in the mad exodus of 1949 nevertheless retained their sense of decency, their sense of propriety, their sense of values? Could it be that others viewed themselves not as Chinese but as people trying to make life smoother, better, more loving for themselves and those around them?

Could it be that they too reciprocated the feelings of the wife of the political prisoner? Could it be that they too were nice people?

Culture Shock

I had heard the words 'culture shock,' of course, but assumed it applied to rubes from Chicago suburbs going abroad for the first time. It was mentioned in the A-100 Class for new Foreign Service officers, but more in passing since it was thought that such people would already have some knowledge and experience in the phenomenon.

To set the context straight for this story, I have to note that I was raised as an Episcopalian. I was even an acolyte in a small parish outside of Seattle, an acolyte until one day a few months after my university career began, and while standing there holding the wine for the priest to prepare, I realized that not only was I a head taller than the priest physically but I was a head taller intellectually. That day was the last time I ever went to church.

As I grew into greater intellectual awareness, I was nevertheless concerned that religion was a fiber that held society together. Without some form of religion, how would people know to not steal, not murder, and not fornicate willy-nilly? We needed religion even if it was not true. It was needed opium for the masses.

On my second assignment in the Foreign Service, I was dispatched to Hong Kong. At that time, it was noted that there were 66 different Christian groups and sects practicing in Hong Kong. Perhaps bringing truth to the poor heathen in that part of the world? Perhaps holding their fiber together?

Shortly after arrival, I made connection with an Episcopal Church program that helped children in need. For a few dollars a month, one could provide support in various manifestations for a small child. One manifestation included tuition for the Episcopal Church's primary school. In Chinese, the term for the beneficiary of this sponsorship relationship is kai-nui 契女 a kind of goddaughter, without religious connotations. The poor little girl, Lee Lai-chun, 李麗珍 was seven or eight years old, her mother was a drug addict, her father had run away many years before. She and her mother lived in a bed space, in the triangular space underneath a stairway in a six-story building.

I would occasionally take Lee Lai-chun out for a ride in my little Triumph sports car, and maybe to a dim saam restaurant or to the New Territories. Or to my apartment where my servant would prepare a lunch for her.

Lee Lai-chun thought it funny that a foreigner could speak to her in Cantonese. Out of her amusement came an idea. Perhaps I could entertain Lee Lai-chun and her classmates at my apartment on the

12th Floor overlooking Causeway Bay. It was not too far from her school. But I would need help since my Cantonese lacked a bit.

In the visa section, the visa applicants are persons who come from many parts of China, though mostly from Guangdong Province. The seventy million people of Guangdong speak an abundance of languages and dialects. The Consulate kept a variety of translators on hand to assist the visa officers in conducting their interviews. One of our translators was a nice looking young woman who had married a few days after I arrived in Hong Kong. We nevertheless found ourselves quite attracted to one another. We became good friends (don't read too much into that phrase, please). We eventually became such friends that I often went to her house, met with her parents, husband, siblings, grandmother, and garnered great insight into the life and customs of a Cantonese family.

Except for the young woman and her husband, no one in the family spoke English. As our familial friendship grew and grew, it was pointed out that my English name just didn't sound right in Cantonese, and the non-English speaking family members found it a burden. The family asked permission to give me an appropriate Chinese name. Initially surprised, it only took a moment of thought to agree. Good idea. On my next visit to the family, it was announced that my new name would be Hui Man-kei 許文祺

Those characters can be pronounced Xu Wen-qi in Mandarin Chinese or as Kaw Bwun-ghee in Taiwanese. Over the decade or two I lived in East Asia, several people have complimented me on the authenticity of my Chinese name i.e. it is not just a transliteration of the English.

I asked both my Cantonese teacher and the young woman translator how to organize this party for my kai-nui and her classmates. We decided in order to explain to the kids why my language sounded funny, it was because I would be Super Clown (超級小丑), a person from some far away place. One of the ladies of the Consulate, Connie Reynolds, heard about the proposal and offered to make up a clown suit for me. The translator wrote out the characters, which we then sewed on the clown outfit. And we invited the kids over for the party. The party was a great success with much laughter and silliness though the kids could not quite grasp that any clown, even a Super Clown, could have such a big [natural] nose and such a funny accent.

The translator and I got to be good friends. Friends. Sitting around preparing for the party, we often talked. I asked her once what she thought happened to her after she died. She looked over at me, and said, easily, and with a little surprise, "Why, nothing."

It was the biggest cultural shock I had ever received. Here was this good and decent young woman without any belief in religion. I couldn't fully grasp or understand her response. Where was the fiber that held together her belief in being a decent person? How and why could she be as she was without some exterior force guiding her?

My amazement that she could be a good and decent person was further deepened some time later. She came over to my apartment from time to time in preparation for some event or another, or maybe just to chew the fat. As I indicated earlier in this story, she and I quite liked each other. On one of those occasions after the clown party, I suggested to her that we might make love. She answered, without animus, that while the love was there, she couldn't and wouldn't because "it would be wrong."

We left our relationship at that point though we have remained friends, and important people to each other, over the years. I haven't seen her in forty years but once in a while, following the old Chinese legend about lovers parted from each other, I still look upon a star and think that she might be looking at the same star.

Wiggly Things

In Hong Kong, the Tai Tong Restaurant, all four or five floors of it, with its myriad private dining areas, was one of the great dining facilities in the fabled Hong Kong of yesteryear. In one of the many delightful side rooms, a mixed crowd of a dozen Westerners and Hong Kong folks were dining at a round table. Perhaps ten or eleven courses, preselected by the host beforehand, were being served. There were no menus. Politeness dictated that one tasted everything and proclaimed it delicious. The second course was a soup, and it was easy for the Consul to assert that it was delicious. It was very tasty despite the oddly shaped bones. The Consul asked with respectful politeness as his hand lifted a third spoonful of the tasteful delicacy, "What kind of soup is this? It's delicious." The host, beaming with pride, announced that it was snake. The Consul's arm froze; he could not move his arm. He watched his arm, frozen in front of him, until his other hand finally reached up gently but forcibly pushing his hand and spoon back to table level. He didn't eat any more of the delicious soup.

The Incident in Guilin

Yi Ar San Sei Ng Lohk 一 二 三 四 五 六   There we were, in Guilin's airport, having just finished a trip down the Li River, floating slowly through the great enigmatic karst formations that have formed the backdrop for so many Chinese paintings over the last millennium. Suddenly, I heard the singsong sound of Cantonese being spoken nearby, and it sounded as if the speakers were distressed. I looked over and saw a family group of six or seven people; a few had started to cry. I imperiously walked over, and asked them, in Cantonese, "What seems to be the problem?"

Their answer may sound strange to you. They were overseas Chinese, perhaps from Indonesia, who spoke no English. Nor did they speak Mandarin Chinese. Further, they could not read either language, never having been to a school in either Chinese or English. They explained that they did not know which plane to take, and which gate to go to. And their plane was purportedly departing soon. They showed me their tickets. I asked an airline representative at a nearby counter where such and such a plane was boarding – in Mandarin. The clerk readily answered, "Gate Number 7." I returned to the family group and, in Cantonese, directed them to the proper gate. Off they went with many thanks.

The story is not over – yet. Guilin is an interior city of China, and a major tourist destination but one does not hear much Cantonese spoken there. The unhappy Cantonese speakers and their obvious distress had attracted quite a bit of attention but no one had known what to do. To use a well-known Chinese adage, it was a clear case of chickens trying to talk with ducks. As the Cantonese speakers hurried off to their destination, the airline representative beckoned me over to the counter. He said, in Mandarin, "Thank you very much for helping."

"But," he added, "It is so embarrassing to have a foreigner translate between Chinese."

The Nose

Perhaps he was too careless about his personal appearance but when he woke up, in his student's family's home in New Bamboo, about thirty miles south of Taipei, the foreign professor acknowledged he needed a shave. He hadn't thought to bring a razor with him since he was only intending to visit a few of his students. But the students' families were so friendly, so amiable, and so hospitable that his journey had stretched two nights longer than intended.

Chinese don't seem to have the same need to shave daily as many Westerners do. Their paucity of facial hair, of course, accented his own unshaven face. And his students were mostly eighteen and nineteen years old, hardly the age for a heavy beard, even if they had been Westerners.

He had been in an accident two years earlier, and the Chinese emergency room doctor had shaved off some of his body hair to treat the injury. The Chinese doctor was completely unprepared for the thickness of the hair and the quantity. It was like each hair was being pulled out individually instead of snipped off by a sharp razor. The discomfort was notable.

In one of those odd but delicious ironies of culture and coincidence, the Chinese character for 'body hair, mao (毛), and the character for 'Mao' Zedong, are the same.

After eating breakfast, and remembering the painful hospital 'shave,' the professor asked his host, with some trepidation, "Golden Student, is there a place in New Bamboo where I might get a shave?"

With a smile, the young man answered, "Yes, there is. In fact, just below our second floor apartment, there is a barber, a neighbor, who surely will be happy to give you a shave."

We walked down the stairs to the street, and there, sure enough, a barber's chair had already been wheeled out onto the public sidewalk, ready for the day's business. With a quick nod of his head, the barber said he would be glad to give a shave to Golden Student's professor.

The professor sat down in the chair a little nervous at getting such a public shave but the barber went out of his way to be polite with friendly explanations about what he was going to do. First came the hot towel, wet, and heavy. The barber carefully wrapped it around his customer's face, tucking it under the chin, bringing it up alongside the cheeks, and folding the two ends together on top of the man's forehead. He patted it down carefully but firmly, and said, "We'll leave this on for a few minutes until it softens your beard."

With the hot towel on his immobile figure, the customer could have been any one of the barber's local customers getting an early morning shave.

Then the neighborhood barber went inside, and the professor sat there, alone, on the sidewalk, in the portable barber chair, unable to see what was happening, unable to move without dislodging the carefully placed hot towel. The main thought running through his mind was the hope that the barber had gone to sharpen his razor.

While musing to himself about his trivial adventure, the professor heard what sounded like three or four boys passing by on the sidewalk, talking and laughing as only ten- or eleven-year-old boys can do. Suddenly, their chatter stopped as one boy said, "Hey, look at that!" The other boys appeared unable to see what had startled the first boy, and as they looked around they kept repeating, "What?" "We don't see anything."

As the boys puzzled over their quandary, the first boy said, "Look at that nose!"

Not wishing to disturb the customer of their barber-neighbor, the boys quietly edged over to take a closer look at the nose protruding out of the hot towel. Unaware the customer was a foreigner, the boys continued with their polite evaluations of the extraordinary nose until some other distraction drew them down the street.

Yaht Yih Saam

On my first assignment to Hong Kong, I had a girlfriend, a girl named Sz Ma-lai. Ma-lai is a Cantonese version of Maria. She spoke English, not an educated English, but a comprehensible English to be sure. We couldn't always get together but would telephone to make our assignations depending on various work schedules. I was a little miffed when one Sunday afternoon, I telephoned her. Her roommate, a girl from Shanghai, answered the phone. The roommate spoke no English, so I spoke to her in Cantonese. The roommate advised that Sz Ma-lai was not home, and it wasn't known when she would return.

The next day, a Monday, Sz Ma-lai and I did manage to meet one another. She was a little upset saying, "You promised to call me yesterday." I was equally upset at her absence, and protested that I had indeed kept my promise to call. Trusting in my truthfulness, Sz Ma-lai nodded knowingly, and said, "When I got home, I asked my roommate if there had been any telephone calls for me." The roommate said there had been one call. Sz Ma-lai asked the roommate if the call had been from a foreigner or a Chinese. The roommate answered without hesitation, "A Chinese."

The left-handed compliment still resonates, fifty years later.

They All Look the Same

It is a cliché, of course, a simple stereotype, a misconception, a testimonial to racial perceptions (or mis-perceptions) yet there is a grain of truth in that inane phrase: "They all look the same."

It seems to be well established among police and like-minded investigators that identifications by persons of one race of persons of another race are notoriously inaccurate, the color of the skin, often blotting out the distinct markers of lips, or eyes, or cheekbones.

A large number of persons have heard, or even used, the phrase, "They all look the same." It almost always refers to someone of a different race than the speaker.

The phrase seems to be a particular commonplace among white people who may feel more at ease crediting this familiar racial misperception rather than owning up to racial bias.

Yet "looking the same" may be more universal than one expects.

At the American Citizens Services counter in the Consulate General in Hong Kong, there is a long counter, perhaps twenty feet long, where American citizens go for passport issues and other problems associated with citizenship.

On one occasion, the American passport officer was just returning to his desk while the Hong Kong employees put several sets of papers into the proper filing cabinet. As he stepped back to his desk in the back of the office, he happened to look up and noticed that the citizen-visitor had left his passport on the counter. He hurriedly directed the clerk to catch the American who had just left his passport.

The clerk, politely, countered, "Which American was that, sir?"

The passport officer responded, a trifle impatiently, "The one who was just here getting his passport renewed."

They both looked in the direction of the stairwell where several persons were descending the wide staircase. The clerk, a pleasant, bi-lingual Hong Kong woman, said, with a tinge of sheepishness in her voice, "I am sorry, sir. They all look the same to me."

Watch Your Dog, Marines

As the Lunar New Year approaches, Hong Kong newspapers, both English and Chinese, carry bold advisory stories warning residents to "watch your dog." The lunar new year, or as it is sometimes called, the Chinese New Year, or even the Spring Festival, traditionally falls around the first of February, the coldest time in southern China. This is also the time many southerners deem it most appropriate to consume "fragrant" meat. Fragrant meat, a euphemism for dog, is thought to warm the body.

There is a team of Marine guards assigned to act as security for the large American Consulate General in Hong Kong. They are armed, trained, and seemingly capable. They had a fierce looking chow dog at the single family home they shared. Yes, you guessed it. One night about a week before the Lunar New Year, someone climbed over the fence at their residence, and stole the dog.

Grace and the Garbage Can

In Japan, there are apocryphal stories about a person falling down in a public place, perhaps from a heart attack, perhaps from something less serious, and people all around scattering, almost helter-skelter, in every direction to avoid a presumed responsibility for the fallen person should the bystanders offer to get involved. It is not so heartless that no one calls for help. Help would be forthcoming but from public officials. And, of course, under those circumstances, there will be a lapse of some time.

Such a system seems so hard, so cold.

In Seattle, when someone falls to the ground, there are often, it is said, several persons who rush up and offer their talents, claiming to have learned CPR at school or work.

Is it that societies of a greater age than ours recognize the onerous burden of helping people outside of the family?

The Chinese tend toward that attitude too i.e. if the deleterious circumstance is outside of one's family circle, it is not a matter of great concern, and not worthy of losing sleep, expressing concern, or worry.

Grace, a young woman from Taiwan, was like that even though her apparent natural sympathy for the downtrodden twitched a bit.

Still, a thousand years of culture cannot be overturned in a generation.

Grace and her Yankee uncle were giving themselves an unguided tour of the top floor of the airport in Seattle. One could look down on the security system, pass by the offices of airlines, the police, the USO for visiting servicemen and women, and watch the first floor people walk hurriedly or slowly about their business.

As the two proceeded down the fairly narrow second floor hallway, coming the other way was a young woman in a military uniform, struggling with a bag slung over her shoulder, a large purse in one hand, and an even larger duffle bag without wheels. As the two moved to the side to let the struggler pass by, the Yankee uncle suggested to Grace that they ought to help the person. Grace demurred, but at the insistence of her companion, who had grabbed the duffle bag offering assistance to the soldier, Grace jumped in. The bags in the hands of three were much easier to carry, and soon were deposited in a not-too-faraway USO. With lots of grateful thanks from the soldier, and from the USO staff.

Grace was impressed with the thanks. And perhaps even more with her own inner satisfaction at having done a good deed at so little cost to herself. Her companion noted that she even smiled, secretly, as she walked back down the hall.

Two months later, Grace, her mother and sister, and her uncle and aunt, were driving in a residential area looking for a particular restaurant. As the car turned a corner, an empty garbage can was discovered in the middle of the street, apparently having rolled off the curb. The driver stopped the car in the street, and asked Grace if she "could take care of it." Grace, having already noted the garbage can in the road, immediately got out of the car and, without a word, picked up the garbage can and rolled it over to the curb and onto the sidewalk. She got back into the car, cleaned off her hands calmly, and resumed her place in the car as we sought the restaurant.

Later, she commented that she probably would not have picked up the garbage can if it had not been for the experience with the soldier's over-sized bag.

How nice to see a thousand year old custom sundered within a single generation.

Cry for Me, Hong Kong

Oh, Oliver Twist. Charles Dickens! Misery!

This is a story, a true one, of a little girl in Hong Kong in the 1960s.

Gone. She's gone now. But maybe she was gone from the start.

When I arrived in Hong Kong in October 1963, I made connection with an Episcopal Church group at the St. James' Settlement, 98A Kennedy Road, Hong Kong side. Through the Settlement, for a few dollars a month, one could provide support in various manifestations for a small child. One manifestation included tuition for the Episcopal Church's primary school. In Chinese, the term for the beneficiary of this sponsorship relationship is kai-nui 契女, a kind of goddaughter, without religious connotations. The little girl, Lee Lai-chun, 李麗珍 was seven years old. Her mother had been a drug addict for several years. Her father, if he had ever been known, had "run away" many years before. She and her mother lived in a bed space, in the triangular space underneath a stairway in a six-story building.

"Bed space" might be a new phrase to you. It meant that one got the space to sleep in for eight hours per day, not more than eight because the next tenant was there to take possession of his space, and then the tenant after him, until it was your turn again. Maybe for the "upper-class" bed space arrangements, one shared the bed space with only one other tenant, giving one twelve hours of respite. And "luxury" bed space meant the resident got the un-shared space for the entire 24 hours. I visited Lee Lai-chun's home once. It was in a multi-story building, dark, and lit only by a hallway light bulb. The triangle under the stairway was enclosed in strong wire so that entry by a thief was not easy, even a thief with a small hand. Since the only barrier to the outside world was the strong wire, privacy was non-existent. One could not stand up in the stairway triangle. Bathroom "facilities" consisted of a wooden bucket. Food storage space was not just sparse, it was negligible. The same small space was used for clothes and personal effects. The triangular living space for Lee Lai-chun and her mother gave new meaning to the phrase teeming cities of Asia, new understanding to Charles Dickens.

With my sponsorship of Lee Lai-chun, I took on some other responsibilities for her. On occasion, I would take her for a ride in my little Triumph sports car. The first time we did so, we drove over to the south side of Hong Kong Island. I thought she might enjoy seeing something other than the teeming metropolis of urban Hong Kong. When I dropped her back at the school, I saw that she had thrown up on the side of the front seat. She had not said a word or made a sign of upset. It was then that I realized she had never before been in a car. Coupled with the twisting roads of Hong

Kong, she had been thrown off her balance. She must have been so trusting of authority, and yet so terrified that she had done something wrong. A half century later, there is an ache for Lee Lai-chun.

Later, when I took her for a ride into the New Territories, I drove with more attention to the special circumstances of my little passenger.

Sometimes, we would go to a *dim saam* restaurant where she would eat sparingly trying to take in not only the food, but also the new experience. A few times, we would return to my twelfth floor apartment in Causeway Bay. It overlooked Hong Kong Harbor, and Kowloon. My servant would fix a lunch for her and she would gently laugh at my efforts to speak Cantonese.

The best, the happiest time, in our short relationship, was on Children's Day. Children's Day in the Chinese scheme of things falls on the fourth day of the fourth month – which also happens to be my birthday. Several ladies from the Consulate helped make a clown uniform with large Chinese characters sewn on the bright red material. The characters were for the words Super Clown in Chinese (超級小丑). We invited Lee Lai-chun and her classmates over to my apartment, which the ladies had decorated, no, festooned, with balloons, and goodies. It was altogether a happy occasion. But to this day, for those little six and seven year old children who are still alive, they have to wonder how even a Super Clown could have such a large [natural] nose, and speak with such odd phraseology. Maybe it was one of the few, the very few, happy days in this little girl's life.

If my own father had not gone away, replicating Lee Lai-chun's experience *a priori*, I might have brought more insight into the relationship with this little child. It would have been so simple, so easy, to have done many more things: include her mother in events; look after her schooling; continue the sponsorship after I left the colony in December 1965. Too self-absorbed in building my own career, I left Hong Kong for my next assignment, never to see or talk with Lee Lai-chun again.

In a much later return visit to Hong Kong, I queried the St. James Settlement folks about her circumstances. They reported that as she grew into her teens, she had gotten caught up with a gang, and had, following in her mother's footsteps, become a drug addict herself.

I am so sorry. So so sorry, little girl.

Case History Form

Child No. 414/S406
St. James' Settlement
98A Kennedy Rd., H.K.

Particulars of the Child

Name of Child: Lee Lei Chun (李麗珍); Sex: F.
Place of Birth: Hong Kong.   Date Born: 29th June 1957
School: St. James' Primary School.   Class: Primary 1.
Progress in Studies: Fair.
Favorite Subject: Chinese.
Vocational Training: Too young yet.   Play/Game/Hobby: Skipping.
Health: Satisfactory.

Particulars of the Family

1. Father's Occupation and Income: The father, who is an earth coolie, is now living with another woman and has 5 children with that woman. He has deserted this family since child was one month old. According to the mother, he has acquired the habit of smoking heroin.

2. Mother's Occupation and Income: The mother, age 44, used to sell vegetables or work as an earth coolie to support her family. Her health is bad. She was hospitalised (Gratham T.B. Hospital) for 2 months last year, and was discharged in Aug. However she still has to have regular check-ups at the Wan-

3. Living Condition: Chai Chest Clinic. In addition, she is also a regular out-patient of Sai Ying Poon Hospital, and at the moment she is again in hospital. As a result, she is unable to (P.T.O.

    a. Type of Building: Old 4-storey wooden tenement building.
    b. Type of Dwelling: A double bunk in the space under the stair very near the kitchen on the 1st floor. As they don't have any other furniture, all their belongings have to be put on and under the bunk.

    c. Number in Family: 3 (Mother, 1 elder sister and child.)

    d. Number of Persons or Families Living Together: 6 families (29 persons.)

    e. Rent Paid (per month): $10.00

    f. Ventilation and Sanitation: Poor. Since it is on the corridor and is near the kitchen, it is rather dark, stuffy and smoky specially during cooking time. Water and electricity are available. Bucket is used instead of flush toilet. Fire-wood is used for fuel.

Remark: The living condition being poor, and the mother is afraid that the child will be affected by her ill health, as well as being unable to look after the child herself, she wanted to send child to a boarding school. This she is unable to do because of financial difficulties - total income from sister (Lee Nui) is only around $120.00 per month. As a result, child was brought here for assistance.

1.65.((.L)

2. (Cont.) work, and have to depend entirely on the income of the elder daughter who is only 15 years old.

The Chinese Ambassador Solves the Balance of Payments Problem

Several years ago, the Seattle World Affairs Council asked me, as a retired diplomat with China experience, to escort two visitors to Seattle around the town. The two visitors were the Chinese Ambassador to Canada and the Chinese Ambassador to the German Democratic Republic (East Germany).

I was happy to do so partially out of a sense of duty to the World Affairs Council, partially out of a sense of responsibility to put my home town in a good light, and, of course, out of a sense of curiosity in meeting such distinguished gentlemen.

Both men were affable, English-speaking, intelligent and polite. As was their bodyguard. Fortunately for the four of us, I had a large BMW 740 that was really a turn-on for the bodyguard, less so for the Ambassadors.

One ambassador related that his Embassy had wanted to buy a new BMW for the Embassy's use. They approached the BMW Company directly, and expressed their interest. The Embassy budget, however, was insufficient for the large BMW 740, and officials said they would purchase the mid-sized 540 model. When BMW officials learned the car was intended for the Ambassador, BMW insisted on selling the 740 model to the Embassy for the same price as a 540, saying, according to the Ambassador, "the Chinese Ambassador ought to ride in our most distinguished car."

In Seattle, the Space Needle is the one place certain to which locals escort visitors. The Space Needle was built for the 1962 World's Fair; it sticks up in the air nearly 600 feet, and is an ideal place to view the scenic city.

One Ambassador and I wandered around the top floor while the other Ambassador and the bodyguard looked at the outside view. Seeing one of those ubiquitous shirts with some Seattle slogan on it, I politely offered to buy one for the Ambassador as a memento of his visit to our city. He declined with equal politeness and perhaps just a tinge of surprise that I had made such an offer. He added, "We can not accept gifts."

Revealing, to be sure. But, thought I, this is the usual Chinese politeness of refusing a gift on the first offer. For those readers not familiar with the process, it is often considered less than polite to accept an invitation on the first and, sometimes, even on the reiterated offer. At the first invite, one demurs, suggesting that perhaps "it is too much trouble" for the host. One thinks of an even more ingenious reason for declining the second invitation.

Upon my second offer, the Ambassador again demurred. I realized that gifting an Ambassador well versed in Chinese culture and contemporary procedures might require some creativeness.

I thought back to my Chinese language course at the Foreign Service Institute in Washington, DC. The four young diplomats, soon to go off to China assignments, were told by Teacher Li Tsung-mi that at a Chinese restaurant no money ever appeared on the table, no bills were ever split up among the participants, and there was gentlemanly competition for one person to pay the bill for all.

The four American students scoffed at the idea each suggesting somewhat strongly that one would soon get burned, tricked, as it were, into too often picking up the tab for friends and colleagues. Teacher Li would not have it, saying that even if the account were out of equilibrium with one set of friends, over the course of a lifetime, or a career, the account would, on the whole, balance itself out. The four students remained dubious. Perhaps three of them are to this day.

I explained this experience to the Ambassador, and elaborated on my own participation in the custom, saying I had spent so many years in East Asia, and so many people had paid for my dinners that my account was way out of balance – in my favor. If he allowed me to buy him this "Seattle" shirt, it would help balance my account, and honor my teacher's observations.

The Ambassador listened politely to the story, looked at me, paused for a thoughtful moment, and said, "Yes. I will take the shirt."

Repudiated. Twice.

Senator McCarthy accused the State Department of losing China, and obliged a number of China-connected Foreign Service officers to leave diplomacy. Many of these people went on to accomplished careers in other fields. One of the principal 'villains' was Jack Service, whom McCarthy accused of being a leftist, a dupe, or consciously or unconsciously sympathetic to the communists. After being fired by the Department of State, and to put bread on the table, Service went to work for a manufacturer on the East Coast, and not long after, he invented and patented a manufacturing process. It was an example of an able mind willing to look at a problem, analyze it, and reach a useful conclusion. Ed Clubb, a noted Columbia University professor and author of several books on China, was another. John Davies, Owen Lattimore, and John Fairbank, were among more than a dozen able persons disgraced and trampled upon by the China Lobby - for losing China. These lobbyists could never face the fact that it was the Chinese who had repudiated the Chinese Nationalists. It wasn't Americans.

When the Chinese Nationalists, often known by the initials of their political party, the KMT, stranded themselves on the 14,000 square miles of Taiwan, they too blamed others for their repudiation by the Chinese population. Perhaps the main culprit in the eyes of the KMT was the student class, a class of people who by education and background had an influence on events well beyond their relatively small numbers in the hugely populous country. As the KMT re-established themselves in Taiwan, they vowed they would not repeat the same mistake.

The KMT would control the student population on Taiwan. They would do so with harshness. Out-spoken students in high school somehow never managed to pass the university entrance examination, and were destined for two years in the army, and denial of entry into the better universities after their military service. Occasionally students who slipped through the university vetting process would disappear, not to be heard from again. And, of course, there were out and out arrests, charges heard in a secret venue, and sentences of three years in the Ban Chiao (板橋) political prison, or fifteen years on Green Island (綠島) where the prisoners were obliged to write mind-numbingly long tomes, by hand, on the wisdom of the KMT's murky political philosophy.

And perhaps most significantly, there was the militarization of the university system.

Near every university in Taiwan, there was a military unit, perhaps a company of 200 men. Just in case. Their presence near the university entrance served as a graphic reminder to university students. There were to be no demonstrations, no strikes, no unauthorized activity.

Inside every Taiwan university, as in the Taiwan high schools, the KMT stationed a military officer. In Chinese, the officer was known as the *Jiao Guan* (教官). While there are no exact English language equivalents, the term might be translated as the Education (Military) Officer. His job, though there were women officers, was to keep an eye on the students under his care. An eye for straying political thoughts, maybe a paper which was not in keeping with the orthodoxy then in force, organizations which were not started by the establishment, inquiring minds asking too many questions, and so on.

In one university, students organized a debate society in which the primary purpose was to practice one's English. A secondary purpose was, of course, to practice one's thinking. One topic for an upcoming debate was "Will a Woman Ever Become President of Taiwan?" The teacher who created the debate topic thought it was simply a debate question about the role of women in society. The *Jiao Guan* thought it to be a political topic. He quashed this public display of freethinking. No one showed up for the debate. No debaters. No audience.

The idea of living free does not belong to the West. It is universal.

Did foreigners lose China?

Take a look at this example. And then decide for yourself.

A university professor, a foreigner, invited his students to go with him on his spring vacation trip to the mountainous east coast of Taiwan. They would take a train from Taipei to the end of the train line in Su-ao (蘇澳). From the train station, they would walk the mile up to the entrance of the Su-ao to Hualien (花蓮) highway. The Su-ao to Hualien road went along the cliffs on the east side of the mountains, the ocean side. The road was one lane, having been carved out of the rocky cliffs at great cost some decades earlier. There was no way for traffic to move in both directions at the same time. Traffic was permitted to flow, in a single direction, at scheduled intervals two or three times per day.

Hualien was a great producer of cement. There was a steady flow of trucks each hauling hundreds of 30-kilo bags of dry cement north to the main part of Taiwan, primarily Taipei, the capital city. The trucks then returned to Hualien empty of cargo.

As the empty returning trucks lined up at the entrance to the southbound one-way road, the teacher approached the truck drivers, and asked if two of his students could ride in the back of the truck toward Hualien. Almost all of the drivers, surprised by the request, amused perhaps, agreed. No more than two persons were permitted, by law, in the open back of empty trucks. Two students climbed up and got in. Got in with whatever small bags they had.

When the hour arrived for the gates to the one-way road to be opened, the convoy then proceeded southward, down the highway, on the narrow cliff-side road. Standing in the back of the truck, passengers could spit into the ocean hundreds of feet below while staring up at the mountains directly above them, and wonder how they had ever gotten into such a glorious situation.

Several hours later, the group disembarked at the entrance to the Taroko Gorge, and the Cross-Island Highway. The students would then walk, occasionally hitching a ride, up the gorge to Tien Shiang (天祥) about seven miles away. At Tien Shiang, there was a small tourist hotel, a hostel, and even space for camping alongside the nearby mountain torrent. The walk through the gorge was spectacular with the cliff–side road cut into the marble-hard rock almost touching the other side of the river.

After a day or two of wandering around the Gorge, the group then stopped trucks carrying the dry cement westward across the island, to central Taiwan, and hitched a ride, on the back of the loaded truck, westward. The ride, especially at night, was spectacular. The westbound cross-island cement carriers most often went at night since the lights of the truck could clearly be seen by the rare on-coming traffic on the narrow mountain road. As the slow moving truck emerged from the coastal clouds up into the mountains, the clouds snuggled like magnificent fingers into the mountain gorges, the stars emerged, unimaginably bright, and shining with a rare brilliance. The wind-whipped east coast of the island was nearly 100% cleansed of pollution, cloud, or other interference between the viewer and the stars. There was no light, only the headlights of the slow-moving truck one was riding in, pointing ahead while the rider sat on the warm cement sacks with his or her back to the front of the truck.

The truck ride continued on across the island, with perhaps a stop in Li-shan, where one could catch a more conventional bus ride to the west coast area, and on to home.

It was on this trip that the foreign professor invited his twelve students to go.

The group was to meet at the Taipei train station at nine on Saturday morning. When the professor arrived at the meeting place outside the station, several students were already there. They mentioned quietly that the *Jiao Guan* had contacted their parents over the last few days, warning them, urging them to not let their son or daughter go on this trip with the foreign professor. Other students, arriving over the next few minutes, told the same story.

The foreign professor thought the trip was sure to be ruined. But lo and behold, eleven of the twelve students showed up, told the story of the telephone call to their parents, told the story of their own subsequent conversation with their parents, told of the confidence the student-child had in the foreign professor, noting that it was the disliked *Jiao Guan* who had initiated the warning, and with the parents permission, agreement, and encouragement, had shown up at the train station ready to go.

Democracy in action. Ordinary people. A student class, once again, as in China thirty years before, showing its disdain for authoritarianism. But not just the student class. The parents too.

But what of the twelfth student? A boy named Alex. He came from a Chinese background. Well, thought the professor, he is not coming.

The entourage boarded the train, and several hours later, they arrived in Su-ao. As they walked up to the gate at the entrance to the one way road, hoping to get a truck ride, Alex arrived, breathless, and said he had slept late, and had to take a taxi, from Taipei to Su-ao!

What had actually happened? The *Jiao Guan* was sure of his ability to direct the students, and the parents if need be. He was supremely confident that as in the debate on a women president at which no one had shown up, the Taroko Gorge trip too would be aborted – on his recommendation. He was so confident of his unquestioned authority that he told the twelfth student, Alex, to stay home and not worry about the trip. It had been called off, *a priori,* so to speak. When the military police that were covering the event noted with great surprise that 11 of the 12 students had shown up, and that the trip was on, they desperately needed their man on the scene. Alex was rushed from his home to a nearby taxi, waiting for him, and proceeded forthwith on the three-hour trip to Su-ao. By taxi.

Alex was a professional student.

Having lost China, in part because of the disaffection of the student class, and having vowed to not allow a repeat of that sentiment to grow in a new generation of students, the *Jiao Guan* recruited volunteers, or even ordered certain students, to do a daily report on the activities of certain persons, among which foreign professors were often included. Volunteer students were rewarded; Alex ended up in New York City several years later.

Nevertheless, eleven of the 12 students, and 22 parents, had voted, voted with their feet.

The May-run Stories:

An Arranged Marriage – Old Style

It was 1910, four years after the great earthquake in San Francisco. The Qing Dynasty was coming to its chaotic end. In the previous half-century, many Chinese had immigrated to the United States, having had great involvement in the building of the western half of the trans-continental railroad. The Gold Rush of 1849 had first drawn them, almost all came from four counties in Guangdong Province of southern China, an area, and era, torn by the broken final years of the Ching Dynasty, warlords, the Taiping Rebellion, and other disruptions of a dying empire. The California influx had alarmed some of the whites who envisioned California as a place for themselves, and their kind. This narrow view culminated in the passing of restrictive national immigration laws which limited Chinese immigration to 105 persons per year (while Europeans had, for half a century, an unfettered path to the United States.].

There were few to call for an Emma Lazarus.

A catch existed, however, which even the nastiness of the prevailing Californians could not overcome. If a person was born in the United States, that person was an American citizen. Every coin seems to have two sides, and the America-firsters were, per force, sitting on their own petard.

The Chinese, or rather Cantonese, emigration path was smoothed by ties among persons from the same village and by clan associations. Many south China villages were populated by persons with a single surname, excepting, of course, the wives who came from nearby villages; it led to the forming of bonds between families, which were very strong and appeared invisible, or at least opaque, to outsiders.

San Francisco had been the major point of entry for the Cantonese for a half century, dating back to the Gold Rush. It was even referred to as Old Gold Mountain in Chinese, and almost never spoken of in some transliteration of San Francisco.

The 1906 earthquake destroyed much of the city's records.

Viola! A person could claim birth in San Francisco, and thus, if one were a Chinese, avoid the unequal and restrictive immigration requirements. By virtue of citizenship, one could even obtain a travel document, and more importantly, the right to enter, leave, and return to the United States without hindrance.

In the years after the earthquake, schools arose. No, no, not public schools but schools designed to teach a fellow villager every aspect of life on a street in San Francisco, a street which had been destroyed in the earthquake. One learned who had lived in each of the houses on a one-block section of the street, where one went to get groceries, laundry, tea, and the other accoutrements of life. Then when one "returned" from China, one could answer the questions of the immigration inspector, "proving" that one had been a person who lived on the street in question before the earthquake. Under the rules of the day, unless the immigration inspector could disprove the claim, the government was forced, *prima facie*, to admit the person as an American citizen.

The new citizen could then return to Guangdong, marry, father as many children as could be logically and mathematically born, thus creating 'slots' for others to utilize afterwards, and then return to the United States, with or without the new wife.

At one time, the Immigration Service estimated that for every Chinese male claiming to have been born in the United States, and for every Chinese woman thought to have been living in the United States, each of the women would have to have given birth to about 800 children, all of them sons.

Virtually none of the births claimed to have occurred in pre-earthquake San Francisco were women; and none of the births claimed to have occurred in China were girls. Hence one went back home to get a wife. Very few were available here.

An industry was born. Not a conventional industry but one in which the *may-run* – matchmaker -- became an important part of the system: finding a wife for the man who came back to marry.

In 1910, a young Chinese fellow who had claimed birth in San Francisco and who thus was an American citizen, returned to his native village in Guangdong Province. It was not far from Toishan City, the main town of Toishan County, the source of about 60 or 70 percent of the Chinese in the United States at the time. He sought the help of his family who readily located a *may-run*.

The *may-run* found a young woman, 17 years old, from a nearby village. The marriage was quickly arranged. The new husband, tarried for a month or two in his family's village, and then returned to the United States. At least one new slot was created in that he claimed his wife was pregnant when he returned to San Francisco though in fact she was not. She had no idea about any of this.

The new wife's name was Tam Hon-ying; his name was Chan Man-kei though in fact he came from a village in which the surnames of all the men in the village were Hui. Chan was his paper name for the slot he occupied in the pantheon of the immigration service.

One thing led to another. The Ching Dynasty collapsed, formally in 1911 with the Sun Yat-sen revolution, but in fact, it had collapsed in south China some years earlier. As World War I unfolded amidst the depredations and chaos of the warlord period in China, Hui Man-kei, or Chan Man-kei as he was known in the United States, continued to send intermittent remittances back home through a village association, which had been located in Hong Kong just for this purpose. The remittance system was reliable and the money meant life-blood for Tam Hon-ying despite the irregular nature of its arrival. She lived with her husband's family, such as it was, the remittances generating a common interest and benefit.

Civil strife on a much larger scale in the 'tens and the 'twenties, followed by the Japanese War which began in China in 1931, not to end until 1945 or even 1946 in scattered locales, and then the Chinese Civil War, and then the era of the Communists with closed ties between China and the United States, meant there was little hope of ... ... why try to put into words that which can not be thought of in words? Contact became a myth, a myth that could not interfere with the ebb and flow of daily life. Tam Hon-ying could not afford the luxury of dreaming about America or joining her husband.

And yet ... bow down to your gods, ye who believe in fidelity, ye who believe in loyalty, Tam Hong-ying remained faithful to her husband of a month, of decades, of a lifetime, a husband she had not seen for years, rarely heard from except through occasional remittances, meager remittances. Perhaps there was a letter written by someone else on behalf of the man for whom literacy, articulation, overt personal feelings were not conventional means of expression.

Through all of this Tam Hon-ying remained faithful.

A cynic can argue that straying women were sometimes stoned to death in the overseas villages of Guangdong Province, and that such a check on some was like the old Chinese aphorism 殺雞警猴 — Kill a Chicken to Show the Monkey.

Yet in 1965 when she came into the Consulate to get her visa, she was 72 years old, and she seemed patient, maybe even passive or perhaps Stoic, taking what comes. How ironic that university students study existentialism when there are so many who live existential lives without having intellectual trappings dressing up their actions, reactions, or thought.

For fifty-five years, she had not seen her husband of less than two months.

Fifty-five years!

Yet she still regarded herself, in her own eyes, as a married woman, as married, as espoused, as a permanent part of another family. Barren of children, bereft of companionship, married to an ideal, which had not, in fact, existed for her. All those years, she had been introduced to those few new persons with whom she had come in contact as Mrs. Hui, the wife of young Hui Man-kei who had gone off to the South Seas – no need to be too specific in those troubled times - in 1910 in a slot of the Chan family from a nearby village. When bandits raided the village in 1934, she was Mrs. Hui; when the Japanese soldiers passed through the nearby market town in 1942, she was Mrs. Hui; when the communists came in 1951, she was Mrs. Hui with overseas connections; when the Great Leap Forward came in 1958, she was Mrs. Hui who could safely leave the village for Hong Kong as a mouth no longer needed and was welcome to depart.

What of Hui Man-kei? Returning to San Francisco in the fall of 1910, he passed the immigration process as Chan Man-kei, and was admitted to the USA as a returning citizen. Troubles in China grew. He continued to send back remittances, anticipating that he would bring his wife, his new wife, to his home in San Francisco. But while the troubles in China worsened, his own economic situation in Old Gold Mountain was not one of abundance. But as life flew by, and yes, it flies by for peasants as it does for those with more of life's abundance, Hui Man-kei grew more and more lonely. He moved to New York, and in his new environment, he decided to seek a wife. He married, settled in with his new wife, had three children, and continued to send back the remittances, sometimes less frequently than other times. His new American wife died after twenty some years of marriage, and after a while, he married again, with another Chinese-American woman.

After the communist takeover of the mainland, with the belated understanding that there were several tens of thousands of Chinese in the United States in false identities, and the words "false identities" carrying an association with spies and secret agents, the American government cracked down on those Chinese believed to be in the United States improperly. The program started off harshly, and led to the suicide of a Chinese-American who had bought an immigration slot decades earlier. When authorities discovered his "false" identity, he was threatened with arrest and deportation. Subsequent recriminations pointed out that he was an otherwise law abiding and productive citizen (as were many of the 'beneficiaries' of the San Francisco earthquake so many years before). A program was then established allowing Chinese to confess who they really were, have it proved in some way, and thereby allowed to "re-adjust" their status into legal American residents, including being legitimately naturalized as American citizens. There were to be no deportations of illegal Chinese immigrants to communist China, and no other country could be legitimately expected to take them.

Hui Man-kei, now an American citizen, a legal American citizen, filed a visa petition to bring his wife of fifty-five years to the United States.

At the American Consulate in Hong Kong, now comes Mrs. Hui, who had married into the Hui village, and had no idea that her husband was known as Chan in the United States. Likewise, she did not grasp that he had married twice, and had several children by one of his American wives.

Seventy two years old, beset by multitudes of turmoil in a century of one tumultuous event after another, uneducated - she needed to mark an X on her visa application form - passive, devoid of any overt signs of anger, angst or animosity, she appeared before the visa officer, cooperative, anxious to help, as perhaps she had been all of her life, not fully understanding all that was happening, having no real grasp of what was about to happen, never having been in an airplane, never having met a foreigner or seen a foreign country, she was about to embark on still another journey, a journey as all of her previous ones had been, a journey decided and directed by other persons.

Mr. Lui, that very able and gentle translator of things Cantonese for several generations of visa officers, was on duty that day. Mrs. Hui, speaking only a rural version of Toishan, a sub-dialect of Cantonese, went through the visa interview calmly, without much overt excitement, and with an amiable, patient manner that appeared to be her way. Through Mr. Lui, the visa officer asked her, "Why, after all these years, are you going off to a new country, to a new life, and to what must be a virtually new family?"

This woman who signed her name with an X, who had never been to a school, who had lived her most intimate moments of life alone, appeared to think a bit, and then thought a little bit more – an observer could see that she might have even asked herself this very question recently. Finally, after a moment or two, she responded, "Curiosity. I want to see what my husband is like."

The May-run Stories:

An Arranged Marriage – New Style

Before leaving the United States for the first time, at the age of 23, the new Consul had pictured arranged marriages as a relatively evil thing with a young girl being reluctantly obliged into a virtual state of concubinage with an older man. Why, for example, couldn't these backward societies do marriage the right way? He'd almost said, "walk down the aisle" before realizing that such a metaphor reflected a cultural bias unwarranted by this brief introduction about his duty to help with his niece's marriage.

Where could love be in a marriage arranged apparently with the main interest being that of the father, with a serious input, sometimes, by the mother? Putting aside his own perceptions of love, which is often defined in Western communities in sexual terms, mightn't it be possible that the parents, portending some love of their own for their own child, placed a high value on what might bring happiness to their own daughter? Aha, you might furiously argue that it is for the girl to make her own decision, reflecting the widespread Western bias towards individuality so manifest even to one's own detriment. Look at the lonesome individuals in Western society, aged, impoverished, alone, in poor health as they come to the end of their days. Then argue against a family unit being multi-generational. Sounds like the argument of a twenty year old who thinks one will always be twenty, free, energetic, and neither needing help nor asking for it. But it goes against the grain of history, despite the successful two hundred years of recent Western history, to think individuality is the great and lasting rule of human relationships.

On one occasion, when in the process of issuing an immigrant visa to the new bride of young Chinese-American, the Consul listened as the new groom elaborated on his journey back to Hong Kong. His father, a Cantonese, had immigrated to America many years earlier. He had five children but only the one son. The new groom was told by his father that the daughters could marry whom they pleased, within reason, but that the son was going back to Hong Kong to meet with the village's *may-run*.

Most villages in south China had at least one person who acted as an arranger of marriages. That person was called a *may-run* 媒人. Being a *may-run* was almost a profession. A *may-run* was often thoughtful, trying to judge the characteristics of the prospective bride and groom so that she could bring them together in a fruitful and successful marriage. More often than not, the *may-run* was a woman. Since girls rarely married within their own rural village (many villages in southern China bore only a single surname), it was imperative that the *may-run* keep and maintain contacts with her counterparts in nearby villages. And like a baseball scout in America, she kept her eyes open for prospects.

In the overseas dispersal of Chinese during the last several centuries, a real industry had developed with *may-runs* arranging marriages for thousands of overseas Chinese during the course of a year, particularly in places like Hong Kong.

When the new groom was asked how he had managed to choose this young woman to whom he was now married, in all probability for the rest of his life, he described the introduction and selection process. The father through a village association in Hong Kong had arranged the assignation with the *may-run*. Initially the young man described to the *may-run* something about who he was, and coming from the heartland of the United States, I think it was Arkansas or Oklahoma, it turned out he spoke very little Cantonese. Armed with that information, and her own experience in such matters, the *may-run* then arranged for a girl and her family to come to one of those ubiquitous Hong Kong yum-cha tea-houses. A private room was arranged. Like a real estate agent, the *may-run* didn't want to present the best prospect at the first interview. She'd show a less palatable girl and family at the start. The interview usually lasted about twenty minutes, and included the prospective bride, her parents, and siblings, after which the girl and her family left the room. The *may-run* and the prospective groom, and perhaps a fellow villager of the father of the groom-to-be, discussed the merits of the girl and her family. If unacceptable, for any reason, the *may-run* left the room, informed the waiting girl and her family of their rejection. The rejection was almost always done with a great degree of tact and diplomacy since the *may-run* could, in a week or a month, want to bring the same girl and her family back for a new prospective husband.

In a side room in the teahouse, another girl and family waited. They were then led into the first room to meet and be introduced to the prospective husband. The *may-run* did much of the talking. The process continued until resolution was achieved.

The prospective groom did a series of twenty-minute meetings all day long on Monday without coming to a positive decision. Perhaps six or seven families came and went without marriage agreement.

The second day, the process repeated itself.

After elaborating on the process, and when asked why he had chosen the young woman sitting at the visa officer's desk, the new husband offered that it is very hot in August in Hong Kong, and this girl was to be the last interview of the day. He thought with the hot weather being so intense, even inside the relatively cool teahouse, the process would just drag through another steaming hot day, and as he opined privately to the Consul, this girl looked acceptable, and he could avoid another hot day of interviews. So, he said, "I told the *may-run* that this girl will do."

The agreement being reached, and both being honorable families, the marriage was begun that night, and the ceremony held a few days later in a restaurant. You understand, of course, what is meant, "by the marriage was begun that night." With the full faith and honor of both families at stake, there was no question of hanky-panky or backing away from the marriage agreement.

It may be that the new groom, anticipating that Americans might look down their nose at someone who had an arranged marriage, perhaps wanted to assert his own manhood through his demeaning comment about wishing to avoid another hot day and "this one will do." It is hard to believe that his apparent casualness was reflective of his true feelings.

And then there was the girl. She was strikingly beautiful. No, no, not the city kind of beauty. A country beauty, unaware of her beauty, just happy to be alive and making her way though life. A thousand grains of rice contributing to the well being of the community. She was like a painting of great beauty one sees in a museum. The sight makes the viewer happy and enthused about life, even after leaving the museum. It was a joy to see this young woman, to see her without thought of personal advantage, to share a moment in her evident happiness.

The Consul informed the two that her visa had been approved. When the new groom went to the finance office to pay the visa fee, the Consul turned to the new bride. Though he had learned to speak some Cantonese, enough to conduct a conventional interview, just by chance the Consulate's best translator was helping on her application. Mr. Lui, an able and gentle soul, was extremely well versed in the Cantonese human condition. So speaking in English, and through the translator, the Consul politely and apologetically noted that Western concepts of love were different than Eastern concepts. And noting that she had known her husband for less than two weeks, might the Consul ask her a personal question to which she did not have to respond? This wonderful country girl, with a depth of politeness, perhaps at being asked a question by an older person, nodded assent. So the translator asked her if she loved her husband.

She looked up in total surprise. Total surprise! Does water run downhill? Is the pope Catholic? She did not have to even repeat the question in her mind. Her answer, swift and true as Robin Hood's boldest arrow, was, "Yes, indeed." A listener could have no doubt of her intent, her belief in her love for this man she had known for less than two weeks and with whom she would spend the next half century.

She and her new husband have ever since become the image of an arranged marriage. Not a punishment. Not an imposition by ambitious or hardhearted parents. Not a program for an old man to find a young sexual partner. Not a heart-rending scene of a young maiden being carried off while crying out to the family she is terrifyingly leaving behind. But to coin a phrase used so often in Western parlance, it was a marriage made in heaven.

The May-run Stories:

Dear May-run:

Dear May-run (媒人):

I am the uncle of Grace Lin Jin-lian, (林 金 莲) that is to say, my wife is the older sister of Grace's father. I am writing to provide additional insight into Grace so that as you search through your lists of eligible young men, you will have sufficient information to provide an excellent match for Grace.

Though Grace was born in 1990, I had contact with her only sporadically until about four or five years ago when she came to the United States to study in an American high school. Since that time, we have come to know each other quite well, and Grace often spends weekends or holidays with us in a suburb of Seattle in the Pacific Northwest. Out in the American West, we are generally more relaxed and at ease with our surroundings than many other persons in America. Grace seems to have adjusted to this change. Grace comes from Tainan, a town in southern Taiwan, a city like Seattle somewhat removed from the frenetic style of life so often prevalent in Taipei or New York City.

That is not to say that Grace is lazy or lacks energy. On the contrary. Grace is a serious minded person with a high sense of duty. Dependable.

There are times when Grace reminds me of the heroine in Pearl Buck's "The Good Earth." One absolutely gets the feeling that she would put her shoulder to the same wheel as her husband, that she would break her back to plant the rice, that she would work all night to make their project succeed. Psychologically, it seems Grace is ready to identify totally with her husband and his projects. She is just waiting to find him, or have someone find him for her.

Marriage will be the biggest event in Grace's life; she understands this, and is looking forward not only to marriage but also to the work needed to make a marriage successful. It is a lucky man who will have Grace for a lifetime partner, and partner is the right word here. Her husband's life will be hers to share in the positive and the not so positive.

Grace is a young woman ready and interested in wifely responsibilities. One can see Grace as a true companion, ready and willing to match her husband's interests. She is psychologically prepared to be a full partner embracing activities of which she has no knowledge. She wants to have children, and is probably expecting to have two or three. She has no hang-ups about the gender of their children, and will happily take what is given. From time to time, Grace has interfaced with the children of visitors to our home, and she has done so with a joy and enthusiasm, which bodes well for her motherly responsibilities. In these respects, it will be a happy family life for Grace and her husband.

Though Grace comes from a prosperous family, it is not a family with the greedy petty bourgeois shopkeeper philosophy prevalent in so many small merchant families. She has a larger vision than such persons. She is not small-minded. Though prosperity has been easy for her and her family, Grace could use a bit more discipline in her financial management practices. She is, however, a good learner, and as she learns, prudence will become her by-word.

Though marriage and motherhood are extremely important to her, Grace also wants to, or will want to, test her wings in the wider world. It is likely that at some point she will want to become employed in a job related to her studies. This could be with her husband's business, whatever it might be, or on her own as an employee of a hotel, advertising firm, a communications company, or a non-profit. It is hard to imagine Grace working in a government office, but it is nearly as hard to imagine her as a permanent stay-at-home mom.

Grace has gotten interested in the political process here in the United States; it might even be true to say she has been bitten by the political bug. It is not inconceivable that she becomes an activist in a political party or organization, or in ongoing campaigns. She is more liberal than conservative though in the main she is pretty much middle of the road.

Religion does not play an active role in her life though Grace is an honest, truthful-oriented, and moral young woman. Despite her upbringing in an orthodox society, Grace seems to think absolutism is an anathema to her approach to life. 中庸之道

Please remember too that Grace is in the middle of her four years of study at a major and highly competitive university in the United States. Her husband should have a commensurate education and education interests. Otherwise, it could be like chickens talking with ducks. While Grace is not an intellectual, she is a curious person not averse to new ideas and thoughts. So too should her husband be.

Grace is like Ruth (in the Bible) and is ready to go where her husband goes, whether it is America, Taiwan, or even some more distant place. Despite her western education, she might slightly prefer a Chinese ambience.

Grace will be a welcome addition to almost anyone's family. I hope that you are able to identify and arrange for her to meet her One-and-Only.

Very truly yours,

Uncle Howie

The May-run Stories:

Dear Wu-fen:

Dear Wu-fen:

Family members have indicated that you are a little disconcerted, although with your usual politeness, that no letter to the *may-run* [match-maker] has been prepared for you. I am very sorry to have left this matter up in the air. Your concern is, of course, quite reasonable as you approach marriageable age.

Let me elaborate on the series of complex and inter-related issues that pertain to marriage, and why your sister got an introductory letter to the *may-run*, and you have not.

When you see a man who is six foot eight inches tall walking down the street, one of the first thoughts that come to mind is that he is a basketball player. If you see a young woman with glasses and holding some books, you might think of a student or a teacher. Considering the huge array of persons in this world, and the even larger number of characteristics that come to mind when you notice a person, the association of characteristics with one individual can vary immensely.

When I look at you, I do not see a junior version of your sister.

Although the two of you share a large number of similar habits and characteristics, you are not two peas from the same pod. You are different from each other in significant ways. And I am not speaking of overt physical characteristics, but of the intangible differences beneath the surface.

Thinking about my supporting letter to the *may-run*, I try to imagine the characteristics that might appeal to the matchmaker in her search for a suitable husband for you.

Traditionally, the major characteristic sought by village matchmakers has been the ability to bear children. This is discerned, often, by a visible characteristic. While there is a word for this characteristic in the medical world, it is a factor not much noticed outside of matchmakers and pediatricians. The word is abduction; it refers to the turning of the thighbones in an outward direction so that a girl's pelvic area can open for the easy birth of a child. This lateral rotation occurs quite naturally in a teenage girl. It is not something you can alter but for millennia it has been one of the highest value characteristics used by matchmakers in sealing an agreement to marriage.

You have had a successful abduction, and if we were in rural China, or we lived a century or two earlier, you would be sought out for this perceived ability to bear children. The characteristic, however, is not so relevant in a world of modern medical science.

Many young women lose their ability to move forward rapidly after their abduction has taken place. Young athletes as they become women, for example, often fade rapidly in their ability to run fast. Yet, oddly, you retain your running ability. But neither historically nor contemporaneously is running fast a high value characteristic in the eyes of a *may-run*.

Along with your running ability, you have a very lithe, limber and supple body. Several family members commented on your dance-like movements when you played badminton with the family last summer. To watch you was like watching a ballet being performed before our very eyes.

Athleticism, suppleness, and grace are not, however, characteristics which matchmakers use to find a husband. With one caveat. There are a small handful of people with some kind of athletic prowess who, if all other things were equal, would hope to find a partner of equal athletic ability – for the children to come of such a marriage. It is nevertheless difficult to persuade a *may-run* to follow this line of reasoning.

You have another striking characteristic, and that too is of no meaningful significance to the *may-run*. It is your voice. Not a singing voice but a voice so rounded at the beginning and end of each word that it soothes the listener, capturing his or her attention almost involuntarily. It is as if you pronounce each word for its full value though at the end, and at the beginning of the next word, you soften your voice so that one is lured into your conversation, listening with rapt attention, not to the words but to the sounds.

In the lexicon of American music, there is a genre known as the story-song. Marty Robbins, the country singer, is known for this kind of song. Listening to him sing "El Paso" recently, I realized I had stopped listening to his romanticized words but was listening keenly to the sound of his voice. Mellifluous, honeyed without being soporific. You have that kind of voice.

Once again, this wonderful characteristic you share with Marty Robbins is not a characteristic a matchmaker looks for. Tough luck, eh?

When I was about fourteen years old, I became fascinated with some articles on the CIA and cultural anthropologists. The CIA employed cultural anthropologists to identify and discern basic characteristics of peoples in different parts of the world. Ever since reading those articles so many years ago, I have tried to observe overt cultural differences in people.

In Taiwan, people walk in two different manners. The Taiwanese walk with a rolling movement, from side to side, almost as if the bottom *sides* of their shoes were rounded, and it throws them a little off balance as they walk. The Chinese walk in a straight line with very little side-to-side movement. Walk down the street in Taipei, and one can almost always identify the person in front of you as Taiwanese or Chinese.

You walk like a Taiwanese. But there is another part of your walk that strikes one in an abstract but nevertheless positive way.

You walk with a degree of honesty that says, "I have nothing to hide. What you see in me is truly me, without pretense or exaggeration." In fact, engaging you in a conversation, one senses a fierce frankness. Trying to explain such guileless honesty to a *may-run* would surely be outside her parameters, and thus meaningless.

You are a very polite person making it a joy to be around you. But how to explain your special politeness to the *may-run* is beyond me, and it may be a characteristic she would assume all of her prospective brides have.

You have an infectious smile, a smile that gladdens those around you. The *may-run* would surely say, "No. No. I don't arrange marriages for girls with infections." So your wonderful smile is no special plus with a *may-run*.

Of all your characteristics, the most outstanding is the quickness of your brain, of your thought process. It is just amazing to watch the quickness with which you grasp a question, an idea, a thought, and leap to the next logical point. It reminds me of a professional basketball player whose eye-hand coordination is so superb, so quick, the watcher has to re-create the player's movements in the watcher's mind so that he can digest what has just happened. You have extraordinary synapses. I have, however, never heard of a *may-run* who has listed rapid synapses as a qualification for finding a husband. Sorry.

As we get to the end of this explanatory letter, you will note that I haven't mentioned your beauty. You are a beautiful girl, to be sure. But a marriage is a lifetime effort, and youthful beauty fades, though it is to be treasured while it lasts. The longer lasting characteristics, the eternal verities like honesty, forthrightness, intelligence, integrity, are, in the long run, more important, more essential to a happy life.

As you can see, maybe I am a little bit in love with you, well, perhaps more than a little bit, but it doesn't obviate my duty to explain why I haven't written an introduction to the *may-run* for you, though I had written one for your sister.

You don't need one, and, in fact, I think you might resent such a letter crowding in on your space.

Most often, the *may-run* wants a much more tangible description of the prospective bride than I can provide. The superb characteristics you have to offer are more internal than a *may-run* can utilize.

You have mentioned once or twice that you might go through life without having a child. That is, of course, your prerogative. But … let me say this based on my experiences and observations in a half-century of life. Don't be afraid to change your mind. I think for a woman to be successful in HER OWN eyes, it is absolutely necessary to give birth, or to try to give birth. It is basic to the nature of life. (And a man needs to leave something behind as well.)

To carry on life is an essential element of the life force in all living creatures.

So accept this explanatory letter with your usual graciousness, accept it as a well-intentioned epistle praising your wonderful characteristics. But I am not sending a letter to the *may-run*.

With very best wishes for a happy and fulfilling life,

Uncle Howie

The Motorcycle Rider's Revenge

It is not that it is a dog-eat-dog world, but in Taiwan it is generally recognized that the larger has the right-of-way. Cars tend to readily give way to trucks; common people tend to give way to those perceived to be more important; and motorcyclists, recognizing this reality, readily give way to everyone except pedestrians. Pedestrians give way to everyone.

He had learned this the hard way too, spending nine nights in a hospital after a car turned left directly in front of his motorcycle sending him flying through the air. A painful but firmly learned lesson.

On another afternoon, he was piloting his motorcycle through the streets of Taipei heading up the way toward the railroad station. As he passed the China Hotel, a taxi turned left in front of him. It would be easiest to think the driver didn't see the motorcycle, and thus give credit to his politeness, not to his rudeness. Fortunately both vehicles were going at a relatively slow speed on the crowded city street. But the driver propelled his taxi well into the path of the motorcycle before stopping, a foot from the now slowed but still moving motorcycle. The cyclist swerved, of course, but it was a close call.

In the Chinese culture, bless them for this attitude, it is generally agreed the first person in an argument to raise his or her voice loses the argument. If force, in the form of shrillness or loudness, is required, it must be because there is no merit to one's argument.

A very nice idea, indeed.

It was a warm summer day, and the taxi windows were all rolled down. One could see two passengers in the back seat.

Stung by the taxi driver's insistence that his size gave him preeminence, as the motorcycle edged by the taxi's window, in a low and very friendly tone, and keeping in mind the admonition to not raise one's voice, the cyclist said, in Chinese, "Your mother and father never married."

At first, responding to the tone of the voice, the taxi driver smiled, and then recognition of the meaning of the words spread on his face. He was not happy, but a quick glance in his rearview mirror reminded him that he had two passengers who were expecting to be carried to their destination.

Helpless he was. Foiled by the smaller. A cheer for the underdog's infrequent victory.

The Incident in New Bamboo

It is probably not a good idea to elucidate on one's stupidness. Unless, that is, the revelation provides insight into another more significant point.

After arriving at Soochow University in '73, he was assigned an apartment in the teachers' housing. Working telephones were not readily available in those units but within a week of his arrival, a working telephone was installed. The quick installation seemed a bit out of the ordinary since other units still lacked phones. For a passing moment, he thought perhaps the security services had had the phone installed. Having a phone to monitor a person was a great convenience – for the security services. But he was a young professor in the Foreign Languages Department, and no longer an employee of the U.S. Department of State. Out with the old; in with the new. No plausible reason for anyone to be suspicious of him. Just a coincidence he thought.

He was forgetting one of the first rules of that old occupation: There are no such things as coincidence.

Not long thereafter, he bought a used motorcycle. It was inexpensive, and compared to an automobile, it never seemed to need gasoline. Maneuvering around the traffic in Taipei was greatly facilitated by having two wheels instead of four. There is, however, more to a motorcycle than sitting on the seat and having someone explain how it operates. But he didn't know that – yet.

Shortly after acquiring the motorcycle, he decided to take a trip down island. Visit a few of his students. See the country from a different angle so to speak. The trip would also provide a chance to more thoroughly familiarize myself with the motorcycle.

The next weekend, he set off for New Bamboo, a medium sized town about forty miles south of Taipei.

He wore a helmet, did not speed, and drove carefully. It was exhilarating with the wind on his face and no impediments to looking around as one moseyed down the crowded road. [This was well before the advent of the high-speed highways that have since become a byword for travel between Taiwan's urban areas.]

Reaching New Bamboo, he was proceeding fairly slowly through the downtown section of this country town. Suddenly he noticed that the traffic light had turned orange, and then red. He reached over with his right hand to squeeze the hand brake. Stupid fellow! He should have used the foot brake, not the hand brake. The motorcycle barely slowed. He entered the now changed traffic light of the intersection as the cross traffic began to proceed through. It was just in time to bump into the side of a small taxi. The taxi stopped; the side of the taxi stopped the motorcycle too. There was a clear dent in the taxi's door.

He stood the motorcycle on its support. The taxi driver got out. The intersection was now blocked by the two vehicles. A crowd began to gather wanting to see this break in the routine of a typical day in a country town that does not otherwise have much out of the ordinary.

The American was well over six feet tall, and more people began to congregate in the intersection, attracted, perhaps, by this oddity. Soon there were about one hundred people blocking all traffic.

The taxi driver was upset, of course, that his taxi had been damaged through no fault of his own. The driver might have expected an argument to ensue. On the other side of this equation, the young professor recognized his own guilt. The accident was clearly and overwhelmingly the foreigner's fault. The conversation now went on totally in Chinese. The taxi driver, ameliorated perhaps by the unique happenstance of having an accident with a foreigner, asked what was going to be done about the situation. The tall foreigner asked the taxi driver how the situation could be resolved. The driver suggested a hefty amount, perhaps the equivalent of thirty-five U.S dollars. The Yankee only had about twenty dollars in his pocket. The foreigner looked at the dent, and suggested a smaller amount, maybe the equivalent of five dollars. The taxi driver demurred saying it would cost a lot more than that to fix the dent. The offer was raised by three dollars. The taxi driver once again began to argue his case when he looked past the foreigner's shoulder, his eyes widened, his face turned white, and he said the five dollars would be sufficient. He snatched the five dollars from the hand of the foreigner, immediately got into his taxi and drove off. The crowd slowly broke up; the intersection cleared. The foreigner started up the motorcycle and proceeded on his journey.

That incident alerted him to the fact that he was being followed, and for the next four years, the security services followed him day and night. Students and friends were asked to report on his activities and attitudes. Sometimes the tail could be discerned; most often not. But it didn't make any difference whether the tail was identified, he was always there, somewhere in the background. For four years. Day and night.

Poetic Justice

As we get into this story, you might well want to ask what a bomb and poetic justice could possibly have in common.

In days gone by, the United States through various agencies, offered friendly countries, and maybe even some not-so-friendly countries, bomb-detecting machinery. Mail, especially packages, could be passed through the machine, and a bomb detected – before it exploded in the hands of some unsuspecting victim.

It was a great boon to those persons in high office who no longer had to worry about being blown up. And, of course, it was also a deterrent to bomb makers knowing that their bomb was likely to be discovered long before it could damage it's intended target.

The machine is placed at the arrival point for the incoming mail; the mail then passes through the machine before being distributed.

You may not know the Finger Game, or thinking that you do, you imagine it is some smutty game played by teenagers. Far from it! It is a game played by business people and government officials. The name of the game refers to the number of fingers held by the Minister's aide on the aide's cheek. With three fingers displayed, it indicates a three percent "commission" or kickback is expected; all five fingers held on the cheek indicates five percent. Thank goodness, god has limited us to ten fingers.

The reasons for the Finger Game are multifold. There is no overt oral discussion, a discussion that could be taped by either of the participants. Similarly, of course, there is no possibility of an upright public prosecutor listening in on a conversation if that conversation does not take place. Likewise for various rivals who might have their own interests in secretly horning in on the conversation, so to speak.

Once the kickback amount is agreed to in the Finger Game, the minister or governor indicates his approval. With a nod, of course.

The next major issue is how to get the money transferred to the minister or governor.

One way is to transfer the funds into the corrupt official's account in Switzerland, or perhaps in Hong Kong. This is not always convenient in societies tightly controlled or where a dominant family or political group wants a share. In those cases where the funds are not in especially large amounts, the money is handed over in another way.

Here is a real life example of business practices often found in East Asia (and elsewhere).

A Dutch East Indies trading company, in business in that part of the world for hundreds of years, bought outdoor sleeping and camping gear in Taiwan. They were the largest single purchaser of Taiwan camping gear for the European market. The company made it a practice to diversify suppliers so that the company was not dependent upon a single source. As a rule, they purchased from three different suppliers. The Dutchman-buyer visited a number of Taiwan manufacturers trying to settle on the three suppliers for the annual purchases.

The Dutchman lived in a second floor apartment in a Taipei suburb.

Shortly after his visits to the Taiwan manufacturers, he would often find a bundle of money, wrapped in a nice package on his balcony deck. There would be no name, no company indicator, no idea of where it had originated. Just the money.

As these annual happenstances occurred, the Dutchman came to believe that several prospective suppliers had thrown the money anonymously onto his deck. Those companies which were among the three that garnered this year's contract thought the primary reason for their success was the money they had thrown onto the purchaser's deck; those who did not get the contract concluded that the amount of money thrown onto the deck was insufficient [and the next year they made an upward adjustment].

Nothing so crude as handling the money over directly.

The scene is now set.

The high governing official was told about the bomb detecting machinery. He demurred. "There is no reason why someone would want to bomb me," opined the high governing official disingenuously. In a more normal world, he was probably correct.

The high governing official declined to have his mail, and especially his packages, pass through the bomb-detecting machine.

Sure enough, those malcontents who thought a bomb would be the answer, worked up a bomb, and knowing of the high governing official's propensity for anonymous gifting, sent him a bomb, a small bomb, which badly, and publicly, injured his hands.

It was an embarrassment for everyone concerned: the high governing official, the security officials both domestic and foreign, the supplier of the machinery, and myriad others.

But it was a good case of poetic justice!

The Dance Hall Girl

I am not a religious person but ever since the 1970s incident with the police, I have really been keen to not only find heaven but to go to it after I die. Just so I can meet and greet the dance hall girl.

Family members will say, " What are you talking about? A dance hall girl? As a diplomat, you've met presidents, ministers, and political, religious, and cultural leaders around the world. A dance hall girl? Have you lost your bearings?"

Is this an old man fantasizing about the proverbial, pure, beautiful, young Eliza Doolittle forced into a situation of ill repute by circumstance outside of her control? Is he like Henry Higgins chasing after a will-o'-the-wisp, a will-o'-the-wisp that does not, in fact, exist outside of movies? Has his imagination gone awry? Is he balmy?

Moralists tend to think people without their particular sense of morals must be people without any sense of integrity. In real life, it is not true.

I have long admired courage as perhaps the most admirable human characteristic. You can not imagine what courage means until you have seen a person, a man, a woman, a student, risk life and limb in a dictatorship. You can not but weep for a man who shows you his hands, hands from which all of the fingernails have been pulled, roughly, brusquely, by an authoritarian thug wanting the names of all of his friends who might hold the same distaining views of the government. You cannot erase the picture of those hands from your mind's eye. Long after the sight, you shiver with the imagined pain.

You weep too for the family of a disappeared student who dared … … dared to do something democrats take for granted: speaking out about something obvious to all except those who think the Emperor's new clothes are beautiful.

How to explain the bits and pieces of courage, which come to the fore from the most unanticipated places? Is bravery a natural part of the human make-up?

The authorities seemed to have gotten it into their heads that I was some kind of a foreign agent. They followed me daily for four years.

It is a very lonely circumstance.

From time to time, a person would bump into me in some context and express interest in being a friend, or showing me some part of the community in which they thought I might be interested. There was an Army major. Occasionally there were young women. And in this case, there was a so-called "businessman" who thought we shared interests in international trade.

"Let's," he said, "go have some coffee and talk."

Since this city did not have those ubiquitous teahouses so readily found in Hong Kong, we went to a facility where there were women whose job was to keep guests company. The establishment was like those in Japan, under which this city had lived for fifty years. The girls came by the table, sat with you, would dance if you cared to, and would engage in small talk, hoping to create a pleasant atmosphere. There was coffee or tea, or a beer or even something harder to drink. The "businessman" paid for it all, ordered the girls to come or to leave.

Having had some experience with this circumstance, it was plain that the "businessman" was a secret policeman, a local equivalent of the FBI in the United States.

I might have known, or guessed, that this gent was a policeman but I never voiced my opinion to anyone.

One evening, back for the second or third time at the same dance hall restaurant, we spent a little time, having a beer, talking peripherally with the dance hall girls – there were two who stayed intermittently while we sat at our table – until it became time to go home. Usually my "host" would arrange for a taxi, often paying for it ahead, and we'd go our separate ways. As we said our farewell, the "businessman" excused himself to take a leak. The two girls had followed us to the door to politely see us off.

Or that is what I thought.

As soon as the "businessman" had left for the bathroom, one of the girls came nearer and said, in a low voice, and in the language of that country, "Sir, you really should be careful. He is not what he seems."

I stood without moving for several moments, digesting what she had said.

Even today, the memory of the sound of those two sentences brings tears to my eyes.

Think what it meant for that girl to risk so much to give me that warning!

Supposing I had been a closer friend of the "businessman" than it appeared. Think what it would have meant to her life if I had told the "businessman" what she had said. She almost surely would have been trashed. Thrown away. So this beautiful person had to make a judgment call. One, that my relationship with the secret policeman cum "businessman" was not a friendly same-side-of-the-fence relationship, that I would not tell the "businessman" of her warning, that I was not a foreign policeman visiting the city.

Secondly, and perhaps most of all, she had to judge that I was a person worthy of being warned. How she made that judgment I do not know since we had exchanged only a handful of words at the table before the fateful words at the door.

Lastly, she had to be a person who disliked, maybe hated, the authoritarian forces that ruled the country with an iron hand.

I do not know the name of that girl; I could not recognize her face if I saw her today; I spoke less than forty words with her. But I admire her judgment; I adore her courage; I bow to her lonely distaste of authoritarianism.

I love that dance hall girl.

A Woman Under a Roof

Chinese write in characters, each character being unique. There is no alphabet. One has to learn each character. It is not as difficult as it might appear to an outsider. There is an idea behind the structure of each character, often tied to its meaning, occasionally tied to its sound.

The characters are known as ideographs. The depiction of an idea. There is frequently great beauty in the imagery of the character, and it is why some lovers of ideography object to the simplifying of the 425 historic characters in the 1950s. It is not just the diminution of beauty but it hits at the very nature of the character.

There is often wonderful logic in the composition of a character, a logic that helps a reader grasp the nature of the word.

Take, for example, the character for *country* a word that might be pronounced 'guo' in standard Mandarin Chinese. There are three components of the character. The box around the edges of the character represents the edge of an encampment,  or as time went on, the borders of an area which eventually came to stand for the borders of a country as nation states emerged. Inside of the encampment were two other components: on the right, a spear representing the capacity for defending oneself; and on the left, a second component that of a cooking fire. It therefore seems a logical follow-through for a student to remember, not the 11 strokes needed to write the character, but the three components which conceptualize the character. Thanks to some long ago greybeard for creating a symmetry and a beauty which becomes self evident in so many Chinese characters.

As the Chinese emerged from the dawn of history, and writing became more and more a necessity, one has to admire these unknown originators for their creativity, harmony, and logic.

But what about abstract words? How to create a character for the word 'love?' Would it be an anonymous greybeard sitting back in scholarly remove? An ardent young swain? Look at the components of the character, not the thirteen strokes needed to write the character. There are four components. The first component is the idea of bringing (… the bride home); the second component is a symbol of a house; the third component of the character for love is that of a heart; and the final component is that of friendship. The concept of the word depicted in the character seems so descriptive, so accurate: bring her to your home, show her love, and end with a lifetime of friendship.

Think of this conceptual preciseness as you imagine thousands of Chinese characters, and then one might understand how it is not just linguistic poets who rebel at the simplification of Chinese characters.

The man woke out of a night's sleep, woken perhaps by the sound of a passing vehicle. For a brief moment, he wondered where he was, and then, collecting his thoughts, he realized he was in his own bed. He did not move, enjoying the comfort of the covers and the warmth like a cocoon around his body. As his eyes opened and he adjusted to the dimness of the early morning light, he saw her, opposite him, on the far side of the bed, still sleeping. He lay still, not wishing to disturb her sleep. He looked at her, thinking of what she meant to him. Her warmth, like the covers, surrounding him with a depth of joy and comfort, complementing his own existence so that the two of them became as one.

Was it the lack of a struggle for family hegemony? Was it her non-competitiveness supplemented by a gentle invisible hand of harmony? Was it because she was Chinese? Could four thousand years of human culture really manifest itself in a single person?

He continued to look at her as he thought back to the Nixon opening to China. It started with a ping-pong team visiting China, the first such visit by Americans in a quarter of a century. There was much comment about the Chinese who reiterated that it was not important who won or lost. Many in the West thought the Chinese were being hypocritical, or if not hypocritical, then inspired by political double talk. But might the Chinese attitude have been taken at face value? He thought of that era as he continued to look at her.

Sometimes, in a crowded room, you might feel as if someone is looking at you. You look around the room yourself, and there, sure enough, a face turns quickly away from you.

As he looked at her, thinking, she slowly opened her eyes, as if she too were wondering where she was, as if she too felt the look of someone staring at her. As her eyes adjusted to the morning, and she realized where she was, she looked across at him, never moving her head, her arms, her body. Then she smiled, without a word, but such a smile of contentment, such a smile of this is where she should be. Then she closed her eyes, the smile slowly, very slowly, fading from her face but the look of contentment remained.

The Chinese character 'ahn' has two components. One component is the roof of a house 宀 and the other component is that of a woman 女. The character means peacefulness.

安

It is not easy to forget this character.

The Theft of an Artist

His father had asked him to go down to the market and get some paper. Despite his fourteen years, Shiao Lu seemed to have an especially good understanding of the kinds of paper his father needed. If the paper was too dry, it crinkled and curled, or otherwise broke into pieces as it completed the process of drying out. It was useless for keeping his father's records. If the paper was moist, as it dried out, even slightly, the ink so carefully placed on the paper shrank until it was sometimes unreadable.

Shiao Lu was not quite average height for his age but he seemed to carry himself in a way both self-effacing and dignified in the same step. Perhaps because his father was the letter writer for those in the market town who needed a letter, the townsmen treated him with a respect that belied his age. Maybe his dignified manner sprang from that respect.

His father had been working on a project to update the *jya pu* 家譜. It was especially important in these perilous times to record the marriages and births in the Lu family if the family history was to be preserved. Two villages not far from the Lu family's native place had recently been burned to the ground; the family records for both the Li and the Wang families had turned to ash in the fires. Shiao

Lu's father wanted to make two or three copies of the *jya pu* so that in the event the fighting went on between the Japanese and the Nationalists, and more villages were destroyed, there would at least be a chance the Lu family records could be kept safe for posterity.

They had kept the *jya pu* safe when the Japanese soldiers marched through pillaging and terrorizing village after village, town after town. They buried it seven steps to the right of the well. But when they had dug it up after the Japanese had passed through, the *jya pu* was very damp, and in numerous places the ancient pages had stuck together. It had taken them many days to carefully separate the pages without destroying the written characters. Some of the characters had been written down three hundred years ago.

The Lu Family *jya pu* went back seventeen generations, seventeen generations of records of marriage between a Lu son and a woman from another village, their children, and then the marriage and children of their sons. Daughters marrying into a new family in another village were not included in the *jya pu* since they belonged to their new family. The surname of the incoming woman was often recorded, sometimes even her given name and that of her native village. This was done in order to avoid marriage between persons who might have an unknown blood relationship.

Shiao Lu thought about the *jya pu* as he headed to the market. If the usual age for the girl to marry was fifteen years old, and she had a child in the first year, as was the custom in their town, then the Lu

Family *jya pu* was about three hundred years old. The *jya pu* must have been created in the last years of the Ming Dynasty when the chaos and difficulties brought on by the arriving armies of the Manchurian Qing spelled troubled times. Perhaps, he mused as he neared the market, some ancestor had thought to do what his father was doing by once again taking extra steps to preserve the family history.

He thought about the idea of writing characters that would be read and looked at by generations yet to come. He mused about the small number of characters he knew, most through the teaching of his father. Their small school had often closed because of the omnipresence of troops passing through or the occasional airplane looking for some structure to bomb.

Suddenly, a shout startled him out of his daydreaming, the voice sounding imperious, malevolent, and rough.

"Hey, you. Stop."

He stopped, looked in the direction of the voice, saw four soldiers in ragged, dissimilar uniforms, one holding a rifle that was pointed in his direction. The soldier beckoned for him to come. Shiao Lu did as told. As he approached the soldiers, he heard one say, "Yeah, this one'll do too."

He was ordered to fall in with the soldiers and they marched away. As they walked toward the edge of the small town, he saw six other town boys of ages like his. They too were obliged to follow the lead soldier. The older boys looked fearful, watching carefully out of the corner of their eyes. They almost looked as if they were looking to run away if they got a chance. Shiao Lu didn't understand what was happening. As they passed by the last corner of the market, the soldiers told the boys to start loading the truck with foodstuffs taken from the market. The boys did as they were told. When they were finished, the soldiers told them to get up on the truck. They then drove away from the village.

He would never see the village again, but Shiao Lu didn't know it at the time.

They drove for about two hours. When the truck stopped, the boys were told to begin unloading the goods into a small military encampment. Then they were ordered into a tent, told this would be their quarters, and to follow orders without complaint.

Shiao Lu was stunned. What was happening? It was beyond his understanding. I have to get the paper for father. He will be expecting me to return. If the paper proves suitable for the *jya pu*, perhaps he will teach me a few more characters tonight.

The Chinese have a number of words for the different kinds of carrying that goes on in this world. One of those words is pole-carry 挑, a single character, a familiar word to many Chinese but which Shiao Lu would learn the meaning of with great understanding over the next few years. Because of his age and his slight build, Shiao Lu was often assigned light tasks as a messenger, a kitchen helper, or as a go-fer. Yet when a camp had to be moved quickly, he was pressed into service as a pole-carrier. The load was often heavy, the pole bit into his shoulder, and Shiao Lu was convinced he would never be able to write again.

For several years, all through his teen-age years, Shiao Lu either acted as a low level servant or as a pole-carrier under great duress. It was hard.

It was unending.

The noise was unending.

The occasional shot echoed in the background. The grunts and screams of the pole-carriers loading what they could onto the ships, the screams coming when the load was too heavy, even for an experienced pole-carrier, and he collapsed to the ground, left to fend for himself, whether he could or could not. It made no difference to the men loading the ship. No one seemed to know where they were going but going somewhere they were. A man in the line screamed that he could do no more. A shot rang out; the man fell to the ground, silent, noticed for a moment, died, and the line of pole-carriers moved on. Shiao Lu, his ragged uniform, torn, blowing in the Yangzi River breeze, was of no importance. He was a leaf born by a wind he could not see, could not understand, to a destination he did not know.

The ship reached Keelung in northern Taiwan.

Shiao Lu who was diffident in the best of times had spoken little since his uprooting from the village, from the small town of his youth, spoke even less on the ship. He did not question. Questions were discouraged.

Once disgorged from the ship, Shiao Lu was assigned to a military barracks not far from Taichung though he did not know where Taichung was, not anymore than he knew where Taiwan was, and not anymore than he knew where he himself was. He ate, slept, did what he was told, involuntarily not questioning his circumstances. How could he even frame questions about issues he had no possible way to grasp, so far outside of his ken, outside of his experience, outside of his learning?

In a garrison community, there is little for the garrison soldiers to do except exist, by their very presence doing their job, a job which was to discourage disharmony by nearby residents.

Shiao Lu lived this way for two decades. No companionship except that of his assigned soldier-comrades. They came from many parts of China; they were older than he was; they had different accents and different customs. They were all lonely. None had a wife. Local women spoke a different language. Communication with locals was non-existent, and it was compounded by mutual distrust of an occupying army directed by an authoritarian group of men. Loneliness was a byword of their existence.

Some, like Shiao Lu, never ever recovered from the shock of their abrupt up-rooting. They had never had a chance to say goodbye to their fathers, their mothers, their siblings, their family. They would never be a name in the family's *jya pu*. They would not be the 18th generation.

They had no way to communicate with their kith and kin. No letters crossed the Taiwan Straits. There was no one to put a sympathetic arm on their psychologically bereft shoulder.

They wandered around, lost, alone, individuals to the nth degree. Few, if any, of these lost men were more than a single unit yet almost all of them came from places where family ties were strong, strong, strong. Important and essential elements of life.

Shiao Lu never ever got over the cultural shock of his sudden and unexpected up-rooting, and if he did, he never showed another person his immense pain.

Twenty years passed so slowly, so quickly.

Shiao Lu was retired from the army. He was given a pittance for a retirement check. It would be a very meager existence for a man who had already gone through a meager existence.

But then, perhaps for the first time in his life, Fate smiled upon Shiao Lu.

The American Embassy operated a Chinese Language School in Taichung. They needed a night watchman. Not only would there be a paycheck, not a large one, to be sure, but the job did not require him to talk with anyone – there would be no one else there except at the end and the beginning of the day – and he could do what he wanted in the intervening hours within the building, left alone to do as he wanted.

Shiao Lu wanted something.

He wanted something to fill the unending ache in his bones, to quell the pain in his heart, something to fill his space in the *jya pu*, something to warrant being part of the 18th generation of the Lu family.

He wanted to paint.

He had dabbled at painting a bit in the many hours of emptiness that the soldier of a garrison has. Now he would have all night, unfettered, un-bothered, un-limited, un-called upon by others. No longer would he be a leaf blown by the whims of the wind.

With the dignity of his newfound position, and the respect that others often extend to those older than themselves, Shiao Lu became Lao Lu.

Shiao is a term often used for young children, and it means 'Little' Lu. The 'Lao' in Lao Lu is a little harder to translate properly into English. On one hand, 'lao' means old. Laotse, a philosopher of antiquity, is often referred to as The Old One. But 'old' in the Chinese custom is a word of respect for a person having wisdom, wisdom often presumed to come with age. Thus 'lao' could be an honorific indicating a wise old man.

Because of Lao Lu's ongoing diffident manner, his quietness as a low-ranking employee, and his quiet love of painting, the foreign diplomats at the Embassy school only slowly came to refer to the son of the village letter writer in some unknown village in China with respect. They did so with admiration and a respect that grew with each new painting, which the few students who learned of his passion, and his talent for painting, extended to this man with the abortive education, yanked by his roots from his home so many years before.

As attention to his painting grew – he painted in the traditional Chinese style, on an elongated scroll with three set scenarios in the painting - there arose a growing admiration for this night watchman turned painter in the closing years of his life.

This village painter, uneducated as he was, knew that oftimes, paintings could lay undiscovered for years, perhaps even generations, to be recognized for their value at a later date. As Lao Lu's painting increased in artistry and beauty, he became even more determined, determined to leave behind a record of achievement that would warrant recognition by the later generations of the Lu Family.

Shiao Lu not only became Lao Lu but people even learned his name, his real name. After all these years, he had his name, a name worthy of entry into the family's *jya pu*.

The 18th Generation.

Lu Xin-zhi 魯信之
Artist

Three Kisses

Love

Well, back in '63, you know I arrived in country, as it were, a few days before her marriage, a marriage I didn't know anything about, and since I didn't even know the girl, I almost surely would not have cared about it except as a politeness to an employee in the Consulate. But as events would have it, we worked together quite often, and often in rather intimate circumstances. No, not intimate in the sense you might mean.

I was an immigrant visa officer working ten-hour days in the Consulate General in Hong Kong processing eligible immigrants from Hong Kong under what was known as "President Kennedy's Refugee Relief Program." The program had arisen out of two concerns.

The first concern involved the refugee Chinese, almost all from neighboring Guangdong Province who had swum, snuck, or floated over the border with Hong Kong as the Great Leap Forward was demonstrated to be the unmitigated disaster that it was. These Chinese were the poorest of the poor; they arrived with nothing. Initially, the Hong Kong authorities had gritted their teeth and absorbed them into the population. But as word spread that if you could make it into Hong Kong, you could stay, legally or otherwise, and when that observation was coupled with the dire straits of life in China with its absurd Great Leap, the refugee exodus began in earnest. Hong Kong authorities realized they could not absorb the desperate population of Guangdong Province much less the peoples of China. They closed the borders. They announced that they would have to send these destitute and poverty stricken refugees who managed to bypass border controls back to China.

Almost daily, ragged bodies were found floating in Hong Kong's waterways as desperate refugees sought unsuccessfully to circumvent the controls.

As these stories broke into headlines around the world, the United States suggested it was untenable that refugees should be forcibly returned to communist China. Both the British and the Hong Kong authorities tartly reminded the critics that it was easy for them to say do this or do that. The outsiders didn't have the problem. Stung by the counter criticism, the Kennedy Administration conceived of an immigrant visa program that would allow those refugees who had relatives of some kind in the United States to become eligible for special immigrant visas allowing them entry and work permits in America. It would be our effort to alleviate the pressure on Hong Kong's resources while showing that we too could do the right thing.

There was a second concern, a concern that didn't quite reach the headlines. That concern was antipathy –- by the Kennedy Administration -- towards American immigration law that had written racial factors into the structure of immigration to the United States. Chinese were limited to 105 eligible immigrants per year. An earlier Congress added the "five" as a sop for those who criticized limiting Chinese immigrants to 100, the number for other peoples from the Asia-Pacific Triangle. And all of this while the annual number of immigrants from "traditional" countries remained unlimited.

Even a person of Chinese ancestry who might have been born in Peru for three generations, spoke no Chinese, and thought of himself as a Peruvian, would be counted as part of the China quota.

While the Refugee Relief Program could ameliorate some of the injustice done by racial criteria, the Kennedy folks continued to work on obliterating race as a criterion for immigration to America.

It was perhaps a fitting tribute to Kennedy that the Congress elected in 1964, in the Johnson landslide election, voted to totally remove racial considerations from our immigration law. And when the new law went into effect with the beginning of the fiscal year on October 1, 1965, I got to sign the first immigrant visa, in Hong Kong, for a Chinese to immigrate to the United States without race being a consideration. It was an elderly woman from Shandong Province in north China whose son had gone to the United States as a student many years before. Under the old immigration law, she would have had to wait in line until some decades after her death before her turn for an immigrant visa would have arrived.

While no celebration took place on that October 1, the Consulate could breathe with a more just heart. Ironic too that October 1 marked the communist National Day, ironic because it had been the communists with their misguided policies that had set in motion the events that lead to the change in American law.

This doesn't have much to do with love.

Interviewing these potential immigrants who often spoke the multitude of languages and sub-languages in nearby Guangdong Province, the Consulate required local employees who spoke these languages as well as English. The visa interview was kind of a triangle with the American visa officer sitting behind a desk, the visa applicant, or applicant and family, sitting in front of the desk, and the interpreter sitting at the side of the desk. A good visa officer looked at the applicant as the interview went on; a good interpreter spoke in the first person, as if the interpreter were the visa applicant. If it were necessary to explain either a question or an answer, the interpreter would express some disassociation with the translation so that she, or he, could ask about, or understand, the issue.

Sometimes the questioning involved intimate details of family life. For example, why did blood tests indicate two of these sons you are claiming as yours could not be children of you and your spouse.

As time went on, the visa officer began to feel more at home with certain interpreters, and thus often sought out a specific interpreter for the next interview. The interpreter began to understand the style of questions the particular visa officer would ask, and the visa officer began to interpolate the responses from a familiar interpreter more effectively.

One of my favorite interpreters was the young woman who had married a few days after my arrival in Hong Kong. She and I became good friends. She invited me home to meet her family, her new husband, her parents, siblings, dog, and in effect I became part of the family. I also had a car, and if the family wanted to go to a rural part of Hong Kong to visit the family temple, I could take along at least one passenger in my little Triumph Herald.

One day, sitting around the living room of their apartment, they explained that it was difficult for the non-English speaking members of the family to use my English name. They asked for permission to find a suitable Chinese name for me. It seemed like a great idea to me – an authentic Chinese name, not just a transliteration of my English name. Two weeks later, after talking it over amongst themselves and considering several alternatives, they "baptized" me, as it were, with a Chinese name that I use to this day.

In studying a foreign language, it is not just the words and sentences that are important. It is the culturalisms that come along with immersing oneself into the way of the language. Using two hands to give or receive something is a long time Cantonese custom. So is declining an invitation until a second or third reiteration. Not using the word four, a homonym for death, is another. No facial hair before one is 60 years old; no pointing of chopsticks when you set them on the table between mouthfuls; pour tea into everyone's cup, not just your own, but be sure to pour tea into your cup as the final act of politeness at the table.

As I took part in the life of the family, the girl and I began to realize that we also had some affection for each other, an affection which began to grow as time went by.

I am so glad for the Chinese antipathy toward public display of affection; there was never any call for us to demonstrate publicly our mutual attraction. There was never a moment of embarrassment to try to gloss over. There was simply no physical manifestation of our attraction.

I was involved in a project for a poverty stricken child I supported through a Hong Kong church. We planned to hold a party in my apartment for a dozen kids. Even though I was diligently studying Cantonese for an hour a day, my language ability was short of the standard needed to communicate with so many children. I asked the interpreter if she would help out, and she readily agreed.

No hanky-panky, just straightforward helpfulness; we even involved several other women from the Consulate.

A week or so after the party, she came around to help clean up the signs and pack away the costumes for use again the next year. As we talked, standing close to one another, I asked her if she would make love with me.

She said, "No."

"Although the love is here, it would be wrong."

But then she offered something else. She offered to kiss me. "With love."

We looked at each other for a moment or two, standing silent in the middle of the living room, and then embraced, followed by a kiss filled with warmth, feeling, and union. I can remember the kiss today as if it were yesterday even though it is 45 years later.

That was the only time we kissed but it was enough to last a lifetime.

Three Kisses
Humanity

To keep the reader from taking umbrage too early in this story, let me first relate the problem at a big textile factory in northern Taiwan, fairly close to New Bamboo, and the current airport. The story took place in the late 1960s.

A textile factory owner who had garnered some big contracts to supply various textile products to foreign countries discovered he lacked the technical expertise from local hires to suitably operate the factory at the standard demanded by the foreign buyers. He had had to hire a number of foreign engineers and technicians to help him get the factory up to the standard demanded by his buyers.

The engineers came for a year or two, and even rolled over into a second assignment, helping the factory operate smoothly and effectively. All was going well, and as the product being manufactured met the standards, the foreign engineers began to go home.

But something happened.

He began to lose his local employees. They quit.

In Taiwan, the government had a policy for years of discouraging students from entering high school. They did this by setting the high school entrance exam at a standard that would limit the numbers of passing grades. This thereby created a large pool of moderately educated young women, with a junior high school education, about fifteen or sixteen years old, who then went out to seek fame and fortune. The usual outlet for this was in a factory manufacturing goods for the burgeoning export market.

The young women worked, often quite diligently, for a few years, perhaps until they were 20 years old, and saved their money, fiercely. In the Taiwan custom, the husband's family pays for the wedding. The young women wanted the money for the start of their new life, a life with a husband, and a family to come. It was a laudable and admirable goal, part of a lifetime plan rather unusual in people so young.

The factory owners asked themselves under these circumstances why were the young employees quitting.

The reason will surprise, and perhaps shock the armchair moralists among you.

Inquiry revealed that the young foreign textile equipment engineers, lonely and far from home, sought the company of various young women from the factory in which each worked. The ambitious dowry-building young women would accompany the engineers offering friendship, as it were, for a fee. An informal system thus arose within the factory society, or perhaps, one might say, the factory family. The foreign engineers who were compensated many times what the young local factory workers made, paid for the companionship, if a reader will allow the use of this euphemism. The young woman earned money to contribute to her dowry, and a happier life with her as-yet-unknown husband, and, a most important 'and', there was no stigma attached, no local folks who "knew" what the girl had done to supplement her income.

As the factory process matured, there was less need for foreign engineers to install, adjust, and operate the equipment. The "supplemental" income of the dowry-building young women fell off, became non-existent. The girls began to seek employment closer to their homes. They quit the factory in which the foreign engineers presence had brought the extra income.

Moralize, if you will, you narrow folks, but let others be in peace.

I checked into the hotel, a small hotel not far from the center of Gao-shiung, Taiwan's second city. The hotel, by odd coincidence, was only a few blocks from where, eight years before, a group of visiting diplomats were shown a flourishing daytime whorehouse right outside of the Mayor's office. Tent-like structures had lined the narrow one block street; men lined up, day or night, paid the equivalent of two dollars, and a moment later, were told what tent to go to. They disappeared into the tent only to emerge a short while later to go on about their more conventional business. This open and public activity was allowed to occur despite the national government's repeated and insistent demands for moral propriety.

As I went out of the hotel to get some dinner, I mentioned to the room-boy my interest in some companionship when I returned, in about an hour. Sure enough, when I returned to my room, a light knock on the door soon revealed a pleasant young woman. In all probability, she was a clerk in a nearby retail store who the room-boy knew, and perhaps had even gone to school with. Here was a chance for the two of them to make a little extra money.

She came in, sat down on the edge of the bed, there wasn't much furniture in the room, and we talked. Then she got undressed and climbed into bed with me. We talked in a friendly amiable manner like two normal people trying to know each other a little better. It could have been a conventional social situation as two persons politely explored one another. No names were exchanged but there appeared to be no constraints on the conversation, easy, pleasant, friendly, and a kind of just-who-is-this-person-I-am about-to sleep-with.

We seemed to like each other, that kind of liking which springs up unplanned, unanticipated, when you meet a kindred soul. It surprises, but it also elates, on a small scale, that there exists another person of a compatible psyche.

We soon, but not hurriedly, went about our activity for the evening, and did so thoroughly and happily, and peacefully, if such a word is not an anachronism under the circumstances. No brutish behavior. Two people sharing an intimate moment in life.

Existentialism. Amiable. Curiosity about each other's foreignness. Resolved for each happily and satisfactorily.

I lay in the bed as she dressed, calmly, slowly. Then as she headed for the door, she stopped, took a step back, leaned over me, and then kissed me fully on the lips. Not a short kiss. A full kiss, a very full kiss, as if there were more than her lips pressing against mine. A kiss that seemed to say I am so reassured to learn that there are decent nice people in the world. Thanks for showing me that you, they, exist. Thanks for genuinely sharing a moment in our lives. A kiss for all mankind.

Three Kisses
Life

    We slept outside in the yard. I used the cushions from the chaise lounge; the children used conventional sleeping bags. We all slept on the ground. It was a pleasant summer night, and an enjoyable revisit to the stars that are so often absent in the interminably cloudy Seattle sky. Yet in the awakening, there was a dull pain in my chest. Probably from sleeping outside on the grass, damp and dewy, and hard. It will pass in a short time, like the sore muscles on the first day of baseball practice.

    But the pain persisted. Finally in the late afternoon, my wife insisted that I go see the doctor, virtually pushing me into the car. The clinic doctors pummeled and listened, tapped and puzzled. Finally they said, "It is strange that the pain in the chest occurs both in the front and the back. That is not usual for muscles. Let's take an x-ray."

    They did, and returned a few moments later, saying that I should go immediately to the hospital, that I should not drive, and should not dilly-dally. Sounded serious enough but when I remained doubtful at their sonorous statement, the doctors said, "You will probably collapse in a short while. Move!"

    Jumpin' Jehosophat. Sounded serious.

We arrived at the Overlake Hospital about fifteen minutes later. They were waiting for us, with a gurney, and I was wheeled into one of those emergency room spaces where the patients await the emergency room doctor and the spaces are divided by what appear to be thin sheets hanging from the ceiling. It was the last space in the row. I heard the man in the space to my left moaning and groaning, and then his wife desperately grabbed a passing doctor, and pleaded with the doctor to do something for her husband. The doctor responded, I can remember his words clearly, "Your husband may be having a heart attack but we have to take patients in the order of need. And the man in the next bed needs immediate emergency care."

I looked to my right. There were no more beds. The doctor was talking about me.

Holy Doodoo!

A moment later, they wheeled me out of my temporary space, and began to ask some questions, the first, of course, being about insurance. As that was promptly resolved, they asked me to sign a form about the operation not always being successful, etc., etc.

Our visitors of last night's outside-sleeping adventure had intended to return to England with my 15-year-old daughter in tow. When I said, "How fortuitous. She will be able to go off, have her visit abroad, return to a recovered father." The doctor looked me square in the eye, and said, "Don't send her!"

Pause.

A long pause.

I told the doctor there was only one conclusion to make from a statement like that.

He nodded agreement.

It was serious. Deadly serious. No glossing over things. No joking around to cover up one's anxiety. Leapin' Lena!

"Okay, let's go," said the doctor.

Funny, isn't it. Just before they began to push the gurney into the cat-scan machine, my wife of two decades, 18 years younger than me, leaned over the gurney, and without a word, in silence, kissed me full on the lips. For what seemed the longest moment. Not a passing kiss. Not a sexual kiss. Warmth spread through my dimming consciousness. Not to fear.

The kiss of life. Sustaining. Warming. Heartening. Life. In the face of death.

Thanks for that kiss of life, woman.

Paragraph

Obtuse. He was. She threw up. Quietly. Without being noticed. He discovered it later after he had returned her to the social worker and the school. The two had gone for a ride around Hong Kong Island. She was six years old. She had never been in a car. She ended up badly too. Ten years later. She never had a chance. Silently. Now silence.

***

The Guangzhou Stories

The Top of the Fang Starring Kirk Douglas on the New Microwave

The American Consulate in Guangzhou, China had been opened hurriedly in 1979 to suit the needs of the Vice President who wanted photo opportunities in China in the event he became the nominee for President in 1980. The Department of State had obliged, moving up their timetable to open the Consulate by a year or two.

As China had not yet fully undertaken the process of modernizing, adequate space in a suitable office setting was, for practical purposes, non-existent. The Chinese suggested that perhaps the Dong Fang Hotel, directly across the street from the sprawling Canton Trade Fair facilities, might be a suitable site, at least for the interim. The Department agreed, and there the Consulate General was located. The visa offices were on the ground floor of the hotel, and the other offices, administrative, commercial, economic, the Consul General's office, were located on the 11th floor, the top floor of the hotel.

American visitors to Guangzhou, the vast majority of whom stayed in the Dong Fang Hotel, were often surprised to discover that the American Consulate was located in the same hotel. They would come up to the 11th floor, snap a picture or two until the PLA soldier standing guard motioned vigorously with his hand that photos of PLA soldiers were not appropriate.

Consulate employees lived in the hotel. The Consul General and family lived in facilities directly behind the Consulate's main office; one had to go through the Consulate to get to their "home." I lived in two hotel rooms just in front of the Consulate.

That was our life. Walk to the office, seconds away. Walk home, seconds away. Go downstairs for breakfast, lunch and dinner.

As with most hotels, certainly in 1980, cooking in one's room was prohibited because of the fire danger. Understandable, of course, but nevertheless, a burden. No hot dogs or roast beef; no apple pie or baked potatoes. No cooking aromas to seep into guest rooms.

It was very trying even though the Chinese tried to accommodate.

We had a microwave oven in the administrative offices inside of the Consulate, an area off-limits to everyone except ourselves. But "Why not," said I, "get a microwave for my room?" Without thinking clearly about the hotel's policy of no cooking in hotel rooms, I asked my colleagues in Hong Kong if they could purchase a microwave oven, a good sized one, and send it up in the pouch the 90 miles to Guangzhou.

With hearty "Hi Yo Silver," the Hong Kong Consulate did just that and a week or so later, the microwave oven arrived – via diplomatic pouch. Joyfully, I toted the big package the thirty feet to my hotel room. Lifting the big box up onto a table in the foyer, I prepared to open the box and check out my new prize.

The door to my room was still wide open as I tore off the packing material, pulled out the microwave, and placed it carefully on the table by the entryway.

There is another aspect of life in Guangzhou in the early 1980s that has not been mentioned. The ubiquitous presence of room-boys, hotel employees whose job was to look after the interests of the guests, and perhaps to report on any untoward activities that might be of interest to public security officials.

As I placed the microwave oven on the table, preparing to see how it worked, the room-boy came by, seeing the door open, he came in, as usual without knocking, and looked at the shining new object on my table. He asked, "What's this?"

"Holy Doodoo." What shall I tell him? I had forgotten about the hotel rule concerning cooking implements in the hotel room. What to do? What to do?

As my confused and befuddled brain tried to work under the pressure of coming up with a satisfactory reply, the room-boy saved the day.

"Is this," he asked, "one of those newfangled TV sets?"

It was one of the few Eureka moments in my life. My eyes lit up, and I turned to the room-boy, nodding agreement.

A front cover of a microwave oven is a bit like a TV set; it has a series of numbers and buttons to push. It is not so far fetched to imagine the room-boy's misperception. Of course, ten years later, there would be no such confusion over a TV set and a microwave oven in China.

It was a Saturday. A nice day. I sat in my room, on the living room couch, with the door open, chatting with several Consulate employees. A person walked by the door, a Westerner. Hearing English spoken, the passerby returned to the open door, looked in, and said, apparently assuming we were connected to the Consulate by our proximity, "Does anyone have a peanut butter sandwich here?"

It was Kirk Douglas, of movie fame.

We invited him in, chewed the fat for twenty minutes, offered a cup of coffee, and relieved his loneliness at being the only apparent Westerner at the Okay Corral. In response to our energetic question about what it was like to film a movie with a truly beautiful woman, he said that when one is filming the scene, each actor is so mindful of the right position to hold one's head in relation to the camera angle that less pure thoughts are pushed aside. But, he added, with a truly genial smile, "After the scene, and after the camera crew departs, …" He left the sentence unfinished, and the breathless Consulate employees cursed their mistakenly chosen careers.

Bluebeard and the Vice President

When we opened up the first Consulate, a Consulate General in fact, in Guangzhou, in 1979, we needed people to fill the positions in the Consulate. Since it had been opened rather hurriedly, and people in the Foreign Service were already in the midst of their assignments in different parts of the world, we had to draft, as it were, those who could cut short their assignments elsewhere without either Department or personal inconvenience.

One day, a new economic officer showed up, introduced to us as Roger Ross. Ross seemed a bright eyed, youthful, energetic fellow who had had a junior level job in Kuala Lumpur. When he learned of the job opening in Guangzhou, he had immediately volunteered, and after some evidently persuasive arguments, had been released by the Embassy in K.L. to fill this job in Guangzhou. The Embassy had been good about its responsibility for the 'good of the Service.'

Malaysia and China are two different countries, two different cultures, two different societies. When you are back in the Department of State, you can often identify those who have just returned from the Middle East. They have a beard, lots of facial hair. Well, not all of them, of course.

Malaysia followed much the same custom.

Roger showed up for his first day of work in the Consulate with a beard, a beard that, if not bright red, was strikingly red. It wasn't a little goatee, or a Van Dyke. It stood out. It covered his whole face. One wit even opined that he must be incredibly ugly if he needed that much hair to conceal his face.

More sober China hands in the Consulate pointed out to Roger, politely, that in the Chinese custom, it was considered arrogant and presumptuous to have facial hair before one reached about 60 years of age. At that age, facial hair was a sign that one had lived long enough to acquire some wisdom. To have facial hair before that age rankled Chinese with a presumption that one was wise when one's age indicated otherwise. This was especially true in the customs of Guangdong Province.

Roger demurred somewhat smugly saying that he understood the Chinese custom but that he declined to abide by their way. He was a diplomat representing his country, and if he wanted to have a beard, the Chinese would have to get used to him, but also to the fact that 'foreigners' from other parts of the world might just do things differently.

"Let them adjust to me," he said pompously.

Before getting to the end of this story, some explanation is in order as to why the Consulate General in Guangzhou was opened so hurriedly. In 1979, as the summer 1980 Democratic Convention was shaping up as a battle royal between incumbent President

Jimmy Carter and insurgent Senator Ted Kennedy, the possibility grew that the convention might come down to neither man being able to secure the nomination.

If the two locked horns, and each side followed without compromise, the convention would then have to turn to a third person as the party's nominee.

The logical third person was the sitting Vice President, Walter Mondale, an able man acceptable to both Carter and Kennedy.

Considering the number of prominent persons who would like to be President of the United States, and the number of persons who actually have a reasonable chance to be the nominee of a major party, the possibility of being the nominee is an opportunity which may knock at one's door only once. In other words, when the potential is there to become the nominee, one must be prepared.

The Vice President and his aides thought they should be prepared 'just in case.'

Richard Nixon had used his China trip with great success in his campaign a few years earlier. China had certainly caught the attention of the American public. The Vice President's office asked the Department of State what events might be happening in China that the Vice President might tap into for photo opportunities

The Department scratched its collective head, responding that there were no immediate opportunities in China. "Oh," the Department noted, "we are planning on opening a Consulate

General in Guangzhou, China, but not for several years since there was still a lot of preparation to be done."

Mondale's people responded that the Department ought to consider opening the Consulate in Guangzhou, perhaps in 1979 or maybe early 1980. They even volunteered that the Vice President would be honored to cut the ribbon opening the Consulate. The Department of State then assigned people to explore a site for the Consulate, and to have a few people ready to "open" the Consulate. The staffers found a large but temporary space in the Dong Fang Hotel. The ribbons were set, the Vice President cut them, and the Consulate was opened with as much fanfare as appropriate.

As we look back thirty years later, we know that Carter was renominated for President (but lost in the general election), Kennedy went on to serve many more years in the U. S. Senate, and Mondale became the Democratic Party's nominee for President in 1984 but finished second in the general election.

Time slips by.

About four months into his assignment, Roger came into the Consulate one day, minus his beard. He still had his mustache but it too was trimmed down to a more manageable size.

"Roger, Roger, what happened?"

Roger explained, rather sheepishly, that try as he might to insist that Chinese adjust to him, the people and officials in Guangdong just wouldn't talk with him. He was unable to get answers to even simple economic questions. He was unable to get the bare minimums of his job done.

Remember, if you will, that the Chinese absorbed, culturally, the Mongols of the Yuan Dynasty, and several centuries later, the Manchu of the Qing Dynasty. Poor Roger never had a chance.

Hunan

一 二 三   A foreigner was walking down a rural road in China's Hunan Province some years ago. He was not entirely sure of where he was. As he continued down the road, he saw two farmers coming his way. As they approached, the foreigner put up his hand in a friendly gesture, and asked them, speaking in Mandarin, "Is this the road to Changsha?"

The farmers looked at each other quizzically; both shrugged their shoulders, and then continued on their way. As the farmers wended their way down the road, the foreigner heard one say to the other, "You know, it sounded just like that foreigner said 'Is this the road to Changsha.' But everybody knows foreigners don't speak Chinese."

Take One for the Team – Chinese Style

There we were. In Guangzhou, China. At a big round table. In the Dong Fang Hotel. In the '70s and the early '80s, the Dong Fang was virtually the only venue in the city for business and government people to meet and eat.

There was me, the commercial officer at the Consulate. The Texas offshore oil delegation, maybe four or five Americans. An equal number of Chinese headed by Vice Governor Zeng, the man who handled offshore oil issues for the Guangdong authorities.

Guangdong has seventy million people.

For a century and a half, Guangdong had been the primary transit and interchange point for ideas, goods, and people coming into, and going out of, China. It was definitely in the *avant-garde* in the pantheon of the late 1970s and 80s. What was tried in Guangdong as China widened and liberated it's economy was, if successful, to be emulated in the rest of China. Oddly enough the Chinese trusted the hundred years of experience the Cantonese had in dealing and interfacing with the outside world. Hence much of modern China's initial contact with the outside world was begun in Guangdong.

As an example of this phenomenon, which lasted well into the 1980s, almost all Chinese words rendered into English came through Cantonese. Words like Peking, Chiang Kai-shek, chop suey, and Gong Hei Fat Choy are but a few of many examples.

The Old and the New mix incongruously in China.

As the dinner progresses, at each turn, one side or the other lifts a glass, the others quickly follow, and the first proposes a toast. "To Chinese-American relations." And then the counter-toast. "To American-Chinese relations."

A few moments later, it is "To the success of the Chinese-American Joint Venture." And then the counter balancing toast "To the success of the American-Chinese Joint Venture."

With fertile imaginations and gentlemanly competitiveness, the variety of toasts goes on and on. Under these conditions, it is best to have any business completed well before the dinner, or failing that, do whatever needs to be done early in the dinner, lest one be three sheets to the wind all too soon.

Not only do Chinese widely observe the long established custom that a person does not drink alone, especially at a table with a dozen persons, but also the full glass must be drunk to the bottom by the end of the toast. The ubiquitous "gum bui" (or in Mandarin, "gan bei") rings out with laughter and in a single language. In these conditions, even Texans can speak Chinese.

The wine and the beer toasts are not so bad but when it comes to mao-tai or gao-liang, it is widely acknowledged one can subsequently feel little grains of sand tumbling about in one's blood stream for the next three or four days. And the likelihood of needing a strong laxative is high.

Governor Zeng and I were sitting side by side. Mid-way through the meal with the Texans, I asked him, "Governor, you go out with the Japanese on Monday, the French on Tuesday, the Americans on Wednesday, and so on. How can you possible handle these 'gum bui' evenings without losing your equilibrium?"

He turned to me, and with a wry smile, said, "I have a secret."

In those days of exploring contacts with the outside world, the Chinese were often very secretive, reluctant to reveal too much of inside circumstances.

My ears stood on their hind legs. "A secret from a high ranking Chinese official?"

Trying not to stutter, nor to show too much interest in his secret, I asked innocently, "What is your secret?"

Keeping his wry smile to a minimum, Governor Zeng said, "I always appoint one of my men as the official drinker for the evening. He does all the 'gum bui' drinks for me."

And with a nod of his head, he said, "See Mr. Wang over there next to the Texans? He does our drinking. I just touch my glass politely."

"Eureka!" What a wonderful idea.

I looked around the table at the five Texans, and choosing one who looked the most vulnerable, I asked him, "How would you like to the represent the United States of America tonight?"

He looked back at me, the only American official there, with pride in his eyes, straightened his shoulders a little, expanded his chest quite a bit, and said, "Ah'd like that just fine, suh." He was immediately appointed the official drinker for the American side, and for the rest of the evening, he matched China's Mr. Wang drink for drink, glass for glass, toast for toast.

All the rest of us noted, perhaps with a little private glee, that sure enough two of his Texas colleagues had to help him out of the room, and guide him to his hotel room. But he upheld the honor of the United States of America, and saved the American official and his own colleagues from a fate nearly as bad as death. He took one for the team.

Big Mac Comes to China

Vice President Walter Mondale had opened the new American Consulate General in southern China's major city, Guangzhou, the old Canton, in 1979. It was located, *ad interim*, on the top floor of the city's major hotel, The Dong Fang.

It was on the open space in front of the 11th floor Consulate offices that our receptions and similar events were held. There was a nice city view for our Friday evening get-togethers with the increasing number of American business people. And it was also the venue for our National Day celebration on July 4.

In 1980, for the first July 4 to be celebrated on the Top of the Fang, as the facility was euphemistically known, local officials and Americans were invited well in advance of the event. With no history of American National Day celebrations in Guangzhou, it was important to get the date on invitees' calendars early.

Guangzhou is ninety miles up the Pearl River from Hong Kong. It is a short train ride, and a very short flight between Guangzhou's Bai Yun and Hong Kong's Kai Tak airports.

Hong Kong overflows with world-famous companies one of which is perhaps America's most noted hamburger purveyor: McDonald's. Our Consul General in Guangzhou, Dick Williams, contemplated how to draw attention to this first July 4 in south

China, the first July 4 to be celebrated in a third of a century. He and a colleague bruited about a number of ideas. One was to invite McDonald's to provide the food for the July 4 celebration. And what could be more American than a hamburger? The two approached the McDonald's company in Hong Kong.

Oil for the lamps of China was part of the perception of foreign business people a century ago. And the syndrome clearly lingers on in our generation. Why not a hamburger for the billion people of China? McDonald's jumped at the chance to provide food for the first July Fourth in Guangzhou. You might say they saw it as a Golden Arch of opportunity.

Arrangements were made. McDonald's would handle the shipment of all its products except the hamburger meat itself. Uncooked meat cannot conventionally be brought across international borders. With a little mental dexterity and flexibility -- on the part of both Americans and Chinese -- the issue was resolved by the dispatch of two young vice consuls to Hong Kong. Their job was to bring back the uncooked hamburger meat. As diplomats, they were not subject to inspection at the border. The plan worked well, the buns, the mayonnaise, and the hamburger meat all arrived right on time. The food was to be prepared in the kitchens of the Dong Fang Hotel, the facility in which the Consulate was located. McDonalds and hotel chefs worked hand in glove for the big day.

McDonalds prepared several big posters celebrating the celebration; the poster from the 1981 celebration is replicated below.

It was a big event: the first American National Day in south China for a third of a century. Someone alerted the news media – perhaps McDonalds – and the US networks and CNN came with full camera crews.

As the guests disgorged themselves from the 11th Floor elevators directly in front of the reception area, they were beset by camera crews. It was quite a cultural shock for many of the Chinese. They were just emerging from the dark throes of the Great Proletarian Cultural Revolution, and to be suddenly thrust into the limelight of western TV crews sticking cameras into faces was almost an unimaginable turnabout.

They had had to pass by a security screening at the entryway to the Dong Fang Hotel; they had had to obtain approval from their work units to accept the invitation from the American Consul General; they had had to dress properly; and they had had to prepare mentally for how to react when meeting the Americans, some for the first time.

Yes sir. It was a day of culture shocks. A day for West meeting East, and East meeting West.

The job of Consulate staffers was to mingle, spreading as much affability as possible.

McDonalds had prepared a large number of Big Macs, their ubiquitous top of the line hamburger. But few, if any, of our guests had ever heard of McDonalds, much less a Big Mac.

CBS asked a Consul to hand a Big Mac to a Chinese visitor. Picking up the styrofoam package with a Big Mac in it, the Consul handed it to a guest. The camera was whirring, getting closer and closer as the TV crew sought to get the reaction of the guest to his first viewing of this archetypical American food. When he didn't react – for some Chinese it is inappropriate to open a gift in front of the gift-giver – the TV crew importuned the Consulate official to ask the Chinese guest to "Open it. Give it a try."

The invitation was made.

The gentleman looked up at the foreigner, looked him in the eye, studied the package for a minute, thinking, evidently, "This couldn't be a trick, could it?" After a moment, he opened the styrofoam packet, looked hard at the sandwich while the camera crew really zeroed in, and then not quite sure what to do, he closed the package, and walked brusquely away, perhaps to take the Big Mac back to his office, or maybe to his family.

And that is how the first July 4 in Guangzhou in a third of a century ended. Happily. Confused. And sometimes chickens talking with ducks.

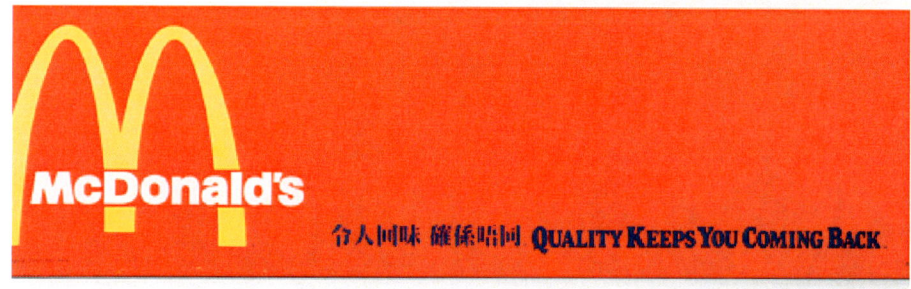

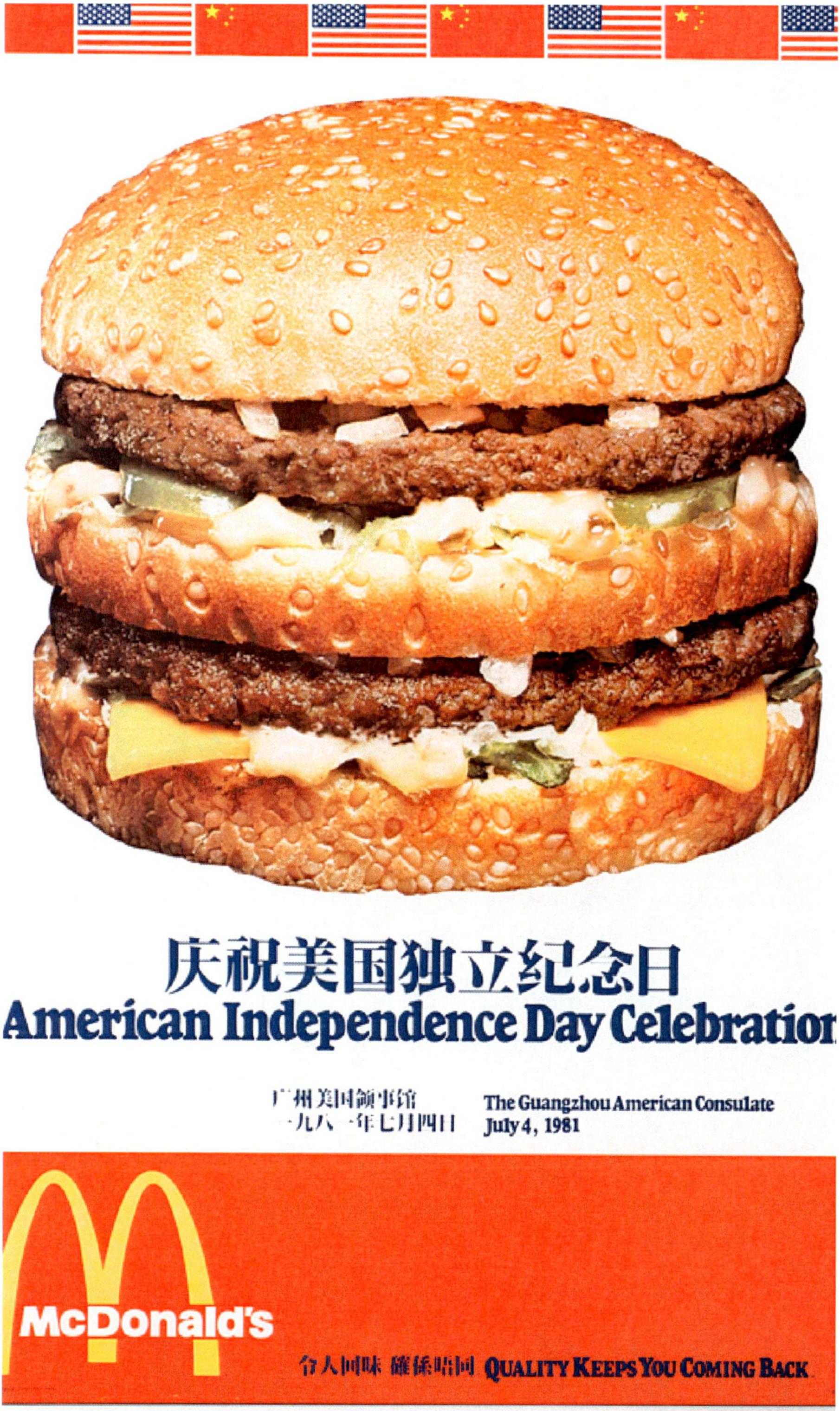
庆祝美国独立纪念日
American Independence Day Celebration
广州美国领事馆
一九八一年七月四日
The Guangzhou American Consulate
July 4, 1981
McDonald's
令人回味 確係唔同
QUALITY KEEPS YOU COMING BACK

Frogs, Aristophanes, Frogs

On one occasion while wandering the side streets in Guangzhou, China, in the late 1970s, the Consul came upon a ten-year-old boy carrying a small plastic sack filled with water. As they walked down the street together, he asked what the boy had in his sack. The young fellow responded that he had some frogs. Taken aback, and thinking perhaps he had gotten them for a school project, the Consul asked him what he was going to do with the frogs. The small boy looked up, with considerable surprise, saying, "Why, eat them."

Good News! Fragrant Meat

Good news can come in many forms, of course. When the large hand-made sign went up at the far end of the huge dining facility in Guangzhou's Dong Fang Hotel, it was, surprisingly, only in Chinese. No English letters of any kind. Rather unusual in the hotel which was the principal hotel for foreign visitors to Guangzhou. Not just "unusual" but odd. And the Chinese characters were not every-day characters. The Consul had to ask what the sign meant.

The answer, and the reasoning behind the secretiveness of the public sign, surprised him. The hotel did not want to offend their foreign guests but they did want to make an important bit of information known to their Chinese, and especially their Cantonese, guests.

The sign translated into English by one of the Consul's local friends said, "Good News" in big bold characters. In slightly smaller characters but just as bold, the sign offered, "Fragrant Meat Season is here." While the Consul understood the words, their meaning eluded him.

"What does 'fragrant meat' mean?"

His friend, hesitantly but gently, responded, "Fragrant meat is the euphemism for dog. The hotel is aware that the eating of dog is repulsive to many foreign visitors, and thus advertises this specialty loudly but quietly so as to minimize discomfort to the hotel's guests."

Maybe Burmese and the American attitudes toward taboo meats are like two people looking at the same coin from different sides of the coin. Each develops a great attachment to a family animal and quite naturally finds it unpalatable as a food. The principles are the same.

The Toilet Paper Caper

As China began to modernize in earnest in 1980, the United States hurriedly established a Consulate in Guangzhou, southern China's leading city. Events were tumbling over themselves so rapidly that virtually everyone was behind the curve, trying to catch up with each new development. In every aspect of life, life had to be reinvented, or if not reinvented, re-established. Laws for travel had to be eased; tax laws had to be established; corporate organizational rules had to be spelled out, and so on *ad infinitum.* Deng Xiao-ping and those governing China, even in good faith, had a thousand questions that must be resolved before the second thousand questions could even be asked much less resolved.

And the China system was a top-down system. That meant that much of the change had to be ordered from Beijing, or in some lesser circumstances by provincial governors daring to look forward instead of marching in place with the *status quo.*

In 1980, it was difficult to find a local official who dared to take the initiative.

There was simply no way all the change in the air could be accomplished without fits and jerks, two steps forward and one step backward.

The American Consulate in Guangzhou was established, hurriedly, in 1979. The offices as well as the residences of Consulate employees were located in the Dong Fang Hotel, a huge eleven story building near the sprawling Canton Trade Fair grounds. The hotel was where the employees lived, and worked, and played. Almost all of the Consulate employees understood that life abroad is different than life in the United States. And that life in a China springing forward into the late 20th Century was different than they had known in other parts of their life, and in other parts of the world.

Each of the employees had made a bargain to live with the reality of the life into which they had been thrust for two or three years.

Large issues or small issues had to be borne with resilience and grit.

The use of the word 'grit' reminds that one of the most irritating issues of life in the Dong Fang Hotel was the sandpaper nature of the toilet paper provided to each guest room.

Nevertheless, Consulate employees managed to bear up well, knowing that soon their tenure in Guangzhou would come to an end, and they would be assigned to Wellington, Rome or Tokyo.

Our Commercial Consul was somewhat less office-bound than other employees, and frequently visited other cities in south China. Guilin, Kunming, Shantou and Haikou were but a sampling. It was on one of his trips to another Chinese city, and another Chinese hotel, that he discovered the rest of China might not have to live under such grating conditions – in terms of their toilet paper – as the guests in Guangzhou's Dong Fang Hotel. The other hotel has soft pleasant-to-use toilet paper.

He had gained some understanding of the way China was unwinding from its past while retaining an awareness of the nefarious ways of bureaucracies everywhere. In the other city's hotel, he went to the bathroom's storage space and got an unopened roll of toilet paper. He noted the name of the Chinese company that manufactured the toilet paper, and their address.

Then he returned to Guangzhou to write the following letter, in English.

> *Dear XYZ Toilet Paper Company:*
>
> *During a recent visit to the fair city of …, I discovered the high quality of your toilet paper in the ABC Hotel. Impressive. I note, however, that your salesman has not yet had a chance to demonstrate your outstanding product to Guangzhou's leading hotel, the Dong Fang.*
>
> *Very truly yours,*
>
> *American Consul*

Stamps, local stamps, were put on the envelope, and it was mailed.

The Consul never received a reply to his letter.

But yes, you guessed it: about three weeks later, a new higher grade of toilet paper was placed, without fanfare, in many of the rooms in Guangzhou's Dong Fang Hotel.

The Kangaroo Kaper

In the late 1970s and early 1980s, there were only three consulates in Guangzhou. There was the one from the Democratic People's Republic of Korea used primarily as a contact point for North Korea and the outside world. We had virtually no contact with them. In the absence of diplomatic relations between our two countries, the Chinese awareness that we had no relations with the DPRK, and in the absence of a consular corps, there was simply no occasion to meet them.

The second consulate was that of Poland. The United States did have relations with Poland. Even in the early 1980s, the Poles were often friendly, amiable, and terribly lonely for company, any company. The Polish Consulate's primary function was to be a convenient point for Soviet Bloc interchange with Hong Kong, the British colony that nominally put great limitations on the travel of Soviet Bloc diplomats into and out of their small territory.

The American Consul General often donated dated copies of Time and Newsweek to the Poles who did not appear to speak Chinese in any way or form but did seem very grateful for contact with the outside world. It seemed the Polish Consulate in Guangzhou, China was at the end of the Polish Foreign Ministry's line of interest.

As the American Consul, I hosted a gathering on Friday evenings, after work – for visiting Americans – in the open space on the eleventh floor of the Dong Fang Hotel, in front of our Consulate's entryway. And not surprisingly, I occasionally acted as a sounding board for non-American business people, people who had no one else to talk to. It was a benefit to us too since we got feed back on their activities as well.

One of these third country nationals was an Australian gent who worked for one of Australia's largest companies. He stopped by to see me each time he was passing between Beijing, Guangzhou, Manila, and Sydney.

On one occasion, on his way back to Sydney, via Guangzhou and Manila, he regaled me with an amazing story. On his way into China, and after having passed through the customs and immigration checkpoints at the Manila airport, he discovered someone had stolen his passport. Not wishing to waste his trip, and already having checked in for the flight, he simply boarded the Philippines Air flight and flew on to Guangzhou, China.

Aware that he had no travel documents, this enterprising Australian nevertheless got into the line for passport control, the line marked for foreigners. He stood close to a group of persons getting their passports checked. He edged around from the right side of the group as if he had already had his passport checked. And then when one of the group moved onward, so did he.

Well and good. He was now inside of China, and thus could move around without a passport. He continued on his journey to Beijing.

He understood that he would need to get a new passport, and once in Beijing, he went to the Australian Embassy to get one. In the late 70s and early 80s, there were not a lot of Australian business travelers to China; he was well known to Embassy officials, and they readily agreed to issue a new passport. But they required that he first report the loss of the passport to Chinese officials. He would need the report to explain why, when departing China, he had no visa, no entry stamp, and a brand new passport.

He duly called on the local police station and made the report that his passport had been stolen in Manila. He got the copy of his lost-passport report, returned to the Australian Embassy, received his new passport, and resumed his business activities.

Late, the second night after filing the report, two plainclothes policemen called on him in his hotel. They said they were not going to arrest him, they were not going to charge him with a crime (for entering the country without proper travel documents), but please, could he explain how he managed to enter the country – as a visibly foreign persons – without a passport.

He explained his simple uncomplicated process. One policeman laughed, the other frowned. And both congratulated him on his inventiveness.

The Mystery
of the Disappearing Business Card

The new Commercial Consul had been dispatched to Guangzhou in time for the twice-yearly Canton International Trade Fair, at the time China's main commercial interface point with the outside world. The Consulate General had been opened hurriedly in 1979, and was located 'temporarily' in the eleven-story Dong Fang Hotel directly across the street from the sprawling trade fair grounds.

The Consulate's large visa offices were located on the ground floor where the immigrant and non-immigrant visa were processed. Most of the American employees worked there. There were a handful of offices on the eleventh floor, for administrative, commercial, representational, and economic purposes.

All of the Consulate's American employees lived in the hotel. All of them ate in the large barn-like structure on the ground floor where the food was served. One could not conventionally prepare food in one's hotel room for a variety of reasons not the least of which were fire and aroma concerns.

In the late '70s and early '80s, the vast majority of foreign visitors to Guangzhou, whether tourist or businessperson, stayed in the Dong Fang. With the multiplicity of languages, and the ongoing issues over Romanization of Chinese names and characters, the hotel management had with some foresight installed two very large bulletin boards where whoever wanted could put up a note, a business card, or even a small sign announcing that such and such a company (or person) was located in Room X. There were no such things as telephone books or directories, and the hotel's front desk was not equipped to handle requests in a hundred different languages and spellings.

Many people were surprised to discover that the American Consulate General was located in the hotel. But there were certainly equal numbers of the thousands of persons who passed through the hotel who had no idea that the American Consulate was within walking distance of their hotel room.

The Commercial Consul often wandered through the exhibitions at the Canton Trade Fair, and would frequently bump into American business people who were unaware there was an official from their own government there to assist his fellow countrymen.

From these experiences, the Commercial Consul thought it would be a good idea to post his business card on the large bulletin board. It had the name of the Consulate, the name of the Consul, and the Consulate's address on the 11th Floor of the Dong Fang Hotel in Guangzhou.

The day after posting the card, he checked the bulletin board. No card. It was gone. He put up a new one. The second day, he checked again and discovered no business card. And the third day, the same thing.

"Aha," thought the Consul, "the hotel contains guests from all over the world. There must be some from countries who don't like America, and who thus remove the card out of animosity." Being a tall Yankee, he thought to put the card as high as possible on the large bulletin board. Yet again, a day or so later, the card had disappeared.

The Consul was a persistent fellow, and he thought to station himself unobtrusively near the bulletin board where he could observe without being observed. Shades of James Bond. Is this what they mean by international intrigue?

What he discovered will definitely surprise the innocent, the naïve, and the guileless.

The card was indeed removed while he watched, twice. Who removed it? It was an American tourist, and then a second tourist. They wanted the business card to show to their tax advisor in order to claim the trip to China as a business trip, and thus write off their vacation travel expenses as a business expense!

Crouching Governor, Flying Tiger

As China began to open up in the early 1980s, there was a steady flow of politicians, business people, and other visitors to the southern city of Guangzhou, especially after the opening of the U.S. Consulate General in 1979. The Consulate did its best to interface with them but it was an uphill battle as this first generation of Americans to re-discover China poured into the country, often with their preconceived notions of what China was like.

Take the Governor of Wisconsin, Lee Dreyfus. He was a genial person, a Republican, a university president, and an intelligent guy. When he led a Wisconsin trade delegation to Guangzhou, after the required pass-through visits to Beijing and Shanghai, he brought with him 100 bumper stickers, bumper stickers that a Wisconsin governor thought would promote Wisconsin in China.

He had toted the bumper stickers all the way from Madison, first to Beijing, then to Shanghai, and finally, to Guangzhou. After the meeting and briefing with the Governor and his entourage in Guangzhou, the Governor eased his way over to the Consul, and reaching into his brief case, pulled something out, saying, "I can't take these all the way back to Wisconsin. People will laugh."

He pulled out 100 bumper stickers that said … …well, it is only fair to put it into context first. Wisconsin is next to Illinois, not far from the city of Chicago. A governor's job, in part, is to promote his state. Wisconsin had printed up thousands of bumper stickers to be pasted on the back of cars, especially out-of-state cars. The bumper stickers said, "Escape to Wisconsin."

The governor had not been in China more than a few hours before he realized the bumper stickers were an immensely inappropriate political comment. The Consul diplomatically accepted the bumper stickers from the governor. In fact, he still has a few around the house. Not much point in passing them out in India, Hungary, Egypt, or Washington State.

Anna Chennault, Chen Xiang-mei in Chinese, was the wife of Claire Chennault, of the Flying Tigers of WWII. Subsequently, an airline bearing the Flying Tiger name was founded, and did a lot of business in East Asia. During the start up of WWII, the Flying Tigers played an active role in the fight against the Japanese. Its leader, General Claire Chennault, was closely identified with Chiang Kai-shek, and later, Chennault's wife, Anna, became closely identified with the Republican Party, and as a Republican National Committeewoman, was a close ally of President Nixon.

Why drag Anna Chennault into this story? She owned some shares in Flying Tiger Airlines. The name Chennault rings a bell with the Flying Tigers of early WWII. Her association, and that of her husband, with the Chinese Nationalists, now resident on Taiwan, paints the Flying Tigers with a certain political coloring. And that leads to this story.

Not long after the Consulate General in Guangzhou had opened, they were alerted to the imminent arrival of the first Flying Tiger aircraft, a freighter, to fly to China in thirty years. One would hardly have thought Flying Tiger Airlines would be one of the first American airlines to fly commercially into China.

Nevertheless, the duty of the U.S. Consul was to go out to the Guangzhou's Bai Yun Airport and help welcome this first commercial flight of Flying Tiger into China.

The local government officials, the airline agents, and the Consul stood out on the tarmac near the main runway as the plane came in. Everyone, it seems, was conscious of the historic nature of this first flight of Flying Tiger into China, communist China.

The Flying Tiger pilot evidently sensed the historic nature of the flight as well.

As the plane came into view, it was flying low, very low, almost parallel with the ground, with very little flight angle. When the plane touched the tarmac at the far end of the runway, all three wheels hit the ground at virtually the same time. A truly perfect landing. Very impressive. The Chinese officials did not say a word, but one could see from the look on their faces that they were impressed too.

ESCAPE TO WISCONSIN

The plane taxied over toward the group of officials, stopped, and shut off its engines. Several trucks drove up. And the unloading of the cargo began immediately.

What was the cargo? It was a plane full of live pigs, breeding pigs, squealing pigs.

From Wisconsin!

The Wisconsin governor had done his job.

And the Consul got to write the report with the best subject line ever: "Flying Pigs Arrive on Flying Tiger."

The Great Chinese Bicycle Race

The first time I went to China was in the late 1970s. We arrived in Guangzhou, from Caracas, well into the evening. We barely had time to get something to eat before the Dong Fang Hotel closed for the night. Then we went to sleep.

The Dong Fang Hotel is located directly across the street from the Canton Trade Fair Grounds. The next morning, we were awoken by the hum of outside traffic. We went to the window to have our first look at daytime China. We expected throngs of cars headed to and from work. There were not even a handful of cars. But there were thousands of bicycles, and there were two traffic policemen standing in the center of the intersection, below our window, directing the flow of traffic, bicycle traffic.

The bicycles were all thick-wheeled, heavy, without gears, very cumbersome and slow. Elephantine. They were manufactured in the millions, apparently for their sturdiness.

If you read this story in 2010, the year it is written, you can laugh, at both our 1970s naïveté, and the phenomenal intervening thirty years of Chinese growth, growth that has made this story passé.

In 1981, I was assigned to the newly opened American Consulate General in Guangzhou. The Consulate had two official cars; the employees, with one exception, had none. We moved around by taxi, or walked, or travelled 'officially' in the office vehicles. Or by bicycle. One of the Consulate employees had a bike. Not a fancy bike but, still, one with thin tires and a three-speed set of gears.

One day, hoping to gain greater understanding of the community, I borrowed the bike, and headed out toward Bai Yun Airport, several miles away. In 1981, there were not many foreigners visible in Guangzhou. I am well over six feet tall, with blond hair, and pedaling the then exotic – for Guangzhou – thin-tired, slim, and brightly colored bicycle, I often drew the attention of my fellow bike riders. No one stared or gawked overtly apparently not wishing to be thought of as rubes or country bumpkins. Or perhaps out of a sense of politeness. But it was evident that they were watching the bike and the tall foreigner out of the corner of their eye.

Several miles from the Consulate, I waited, along with fifty or more other cyclists, for the traffic light to change. As it turned green, we all surged ahead, politely enough, to be sure. I noticed one young man who appeared to be quite well-built, pedaling his bike energetically, clearly attempting to keep ahead of me yet without appearing to race. He pedaled fast, then faster. As I realized what was happening I accepted the unstated challenge, the unstated invitation to be the first up the small hill on the way to the airport. As I began to get up to speed, I realized it was time to shift gears, a process which is done virtually with a flick of the finger.

I immediately felt the increased speed as I shifted into second gear. As we, the young man and the forty-year old foreigner, picked up speed and reached the brow of the small rise, I shifted into third gear. The young Chinese racer was now pedaling his bike furiously, rapidly, and he looked over to see if I was still alongside of him. As I eased into third gear, and began pedaling firmly but easily, the young Chinese began to fall back, or perhaps, it was I who began to edge well into the lead.

I can still remember the look on his face, as he watched mystified, stunned, and surprised as I pedaled easily past him and into the lead. He surely had not lost many races. But he finished in second place on the way to the Bai Yun airport on that day in 1981.

It's Cold South of the Yangzi River

At the [early] Spring Canton Trade Fair, China's twice-a-year international exhibition, the Consul was talking with some traders from China's far northeast, where winter temperatures frequently, and for long periods of time, hover around zero degrees. The Consul opined that the traders from Manchuria must be very happy to come south in the middle of winter. Several of them looked up in surprise, saying, "No. No. It is so cold here in Guangzhou that it borders on the truly uncomfortable."

They went on to explain that north of the Yangzi River, almost all cities have central heating systems that make life bearable, even in the extreme winters of North China. South of the Yangzi River the weather is deemed to be not sufficiently cold to warrant central heating. It is a rare southern city that utilizes central heating. Consequently, in the cool-to-cold temperatures that prevail in southern China, Northerners freeze.

The Handy Official

Upon entering the Foreign Service, new employees are assigned to an eight-week course familiarizing themselves with government procedures and regulations. They are also introduced to other government agencies with which they may interface in their work in Embassies and Consulates, and with the myriad complications and customs one might run into as the new employees spread out around the world.

The introductory course could be a small or large culture shock depending upon the individual's familiarity with both government institutions and with the plethora of customs in different parts of our planet.

One example of how to grasp the cultural gulfs that exist between the different peoples of the world is the story of the American woman who asked the Indian woman, "Why do you wear diamonds in your nose?" Though a bit intrusive, it was a completely innocent and sincere question intended to be taken at face value. The Indian woman, wanting to be polite, sincere and friendly in turn, responded, "Because I like them better than rubies." Each woman was being sincere, honest, and forthcoming though each attached different meaning to the same words.

Another example, and one which seemed to strike the new diplomats most saliently, was the situation posed by the course instructor: What do you do, if at a reception or a diplomatic event, the Deputy Foreign Minister of your host country dances very closely with your wife, and maybe even places his hand on her posterior?

It was a real question for the beginning diplomats. With thirty young persons from a wide range of backgrounds, the answers to the instructor's question were, of course, varied. After listening to the diverse suggested reactions, the instructor summed up his advice in a single sentence: "Whatever you do, do not create a scene."

Make up a reason to leave, think of a presumed illness, or even the ubiquitous "got to get home to the baby-sitter." But above all, be diplomatic. Do not create an incident.

An American diplomat had invited a non-English speaking Chinese official to dine with him in the Dong Fang Hotel's finest restaurant. At the time, the venue was thought to be perhaps the best place in Guangzhou.

The diplomat's partner, a woman who spoke Chinese as her native language but was not from the PRC, joined them. She could cover for the diplomat's shortcomings in Chinese thereby facilitating the conversation, one of the earliest informal conversations to take place between officials in south China.

The American and the Chinese sat opposite each other at a rectangular table. The American's partner, the lady who spoke

Chinese, sat next to the Chinese gent so she could, if necessary, assist more easily in the communication between the two officials.

The dinner, and the exploratory conversation, went on with apparent conviviality, until, as the waiter carried off the last of the empty plates, the lady said, in English, that she would like to go. When the diplomat said he had a few more things he wanted to talk about with the Chinese official, she responded that she really would like to go. Once again, the rather dense American official demurred. The American's partner then said though without raising the sound of her voice but intensifying it substantially, "I would really like to go now." The 'now' was pronounced quite fervently.

"Aha," thought the diplomat, "some problem has arisen. She has to go to the bathroom. Maybe she is going to be sick. Maybe it is that time of the month."

Dense fellow, the American. After they quickly signed for the bill, and hurried off to their residence in the hotel, the diplomat's partner, a refined and polite lady under normal circumstances, furiously and angrily complained that the Chinese official had persistently placed his hand on her knee, then her thigh, until she could no longer abide his rudeness, even for diplomatic gain.

The dense American, finally catching a glimmer, no, more than a glimmer, of what had been going on, apologized to his partner, and the two went off, the partner somewhat mollified, to their next foray into international diplomacy.

How We Stopped the Suicide of the Consul

A small Embassy or Consulate can be an idyllic time for Embassy or Consulate staffers – if they get on with one another. If they don't get on well, or if there is one onion among the petunias, the usual two years can seem half of eternity causing one to think of one's profession as an albatross.

"Why didn't I stay with Goldman Sachs?"

"Why didn't I continue to teach?"

In a small post, one is dependent upon one's colleagues for the everyday congeniality that is often extended between workmates, colleagues and friends. It is sometimes difficult to properly measure friends in the local community. Can one take their professions of friendship at face value? Of course, many of those friendships are genuine. There are so many nice people in every corner of the planet. But you don't *know!*

You do *know* about the trustworthiness of your colleagues.

The Ambassador, or Consul General, in a small post is usually well aware of this syndrome. Many principal officers seek to ameliorate the condition by various means: invitations to dinner that are social, not professional; the celebration of obscure American holidays; assignments to look into conditions in another part of the consular district; transporting the diplomatic pouch to a larger embassy; inclusion in a small dinner for a visiting important or famous person; and so on.

Guangzhou, China was one of those posts. It had just been opened, in 1979, opened in a strange country, with relationships unsure, with language gulfs forming immense barriers, especially for non-language personnel, food and travel procedures different than the staffers were used to.

The Consulate offices, except for the visa section on the ground floor, were located on the top floor of a hotel, at the time the only suitable facility in Guangzhou. The hotel was the residence for all the employees. The Consul General's residence where the CG, his spouse, and their two teen-age children lived was immediately adjacent to the Consulate offices. Dinner guests and other family visitors had to pass through the Consulate offices to get to the Consul General's home.

The staffers ate in a large communal dining hall where one could find, for a time, little notes posted on a bulletin board near the entry that said, "Will the guest who left 37 cents on Table 48 Tuesday night please come and pick it up?" Tipping is those days of communist zealotry was taboo, a sign of decadence.

There was, of course, a General Services officer (GSO). His name, oddly enough, was Carleton Fisk, like the baseball player. His responsibilities included arranging for those myriad things that make life go smoothly for employees - a microwave oven, books, those extraneous things which could make one's hotel room seem at least halfway livable, working typewriters, suitable staffing in a city where there was no immediate history of working for foreigners and at foreign standards.

It was a thankless job; there was simply no way the job could be done to everyone's satisfaction. The GSO's inability to do the job caused some grumbling among the employees. Finally one vice consul at his wit's end (and you can read that both ways) drafted up an unclassified telegram purportedly from the Department of State and telegraphed to the Consulate General in Guangzhou. The worldwide message congratulated Mr. Carleton Fisk for being the "Administrative Officer of the Year", for the entire Department of State. The witty gent slipped it into the Unclassified Reading Folder that each employee was supposed to read at least once a week, usually on Friday afternoons.

Then he hid behind a nearby doorway waiting for employees to read the missive. As employees read the file, there were groans, moans, oaths, and general expressions of chagrin. But the best response was from the employee who muttered, "My God, if this is true, I am resigning from the Foreign Service."

Nevertheless, such manifestations of humor, of good spiritedness, were the things that helped the Consulate employees through their two years in Guangzhou.

Please note the intentional avoidance of the phrase 'gallows humor.'

The Consul General, our first representative in Guangzhou in more than thirty years, was a genial sort, who in his younger days had been one of the Quiz Kids on national radio. His name was Dick Williams, and he later became Ambassador to Mongolia and to Singapore and was the Consul General in Hong Kong (one of our largest consulates general). Dick and Jane had two children. One, Maria, was an energetic, thoughtful teenager about 14 years old.

Our new Commercial officer, Jacques David, had had a checkered career in the Foreign Service, and had returned to government service with the Department of Commerce - after a hiatus of several years. Commerce was setting up the new U S Foreign Commercial Service, and Jacques was in the forefront of their effort, both worldwide and in China. Funding for new organizations within a bureaucracy is initially often patchwork and even erratic.

The diplomatic pouch, with mail and messages from the U.S., came to Guangzhou once a week.

One day, as Jacques was in his office reading his newly arrived mail, Maria came out of the family's apartment in the rear of the Consulate, and purposefully bounced in her unique bubbly manner into Jacques' office.

"How's it going?"

"Are you going to Hong Kong this weekend?" she asked with youthful enthusiasm.

Jacques seemed depressed. Very depressed.

Maria just laughed. Or was it a giggle?

Jacques, with his eyes lowered, seemed to be focusing on a particular piece of mail, and without looking up, said morosely, "Not now, Maria. I am not in the mood for horseplay."

With that Maria smiled her effervescent best, laughed, and said, "Okay, I'm out of here."

She actually had the audacity to skip on her way out of Jacques' office. Perhaps her father had never talked to her about the negative effects of an unhappy Consulate.

When Jacques realized she had thankfully gone, he looked down at the letter in his hand, from the Department of Commerce. The letter said, "Due to budgetary constraints, we no longer have funds for your position in Guangzhou. Your position will be abolished. We will endeavor to make arrangements in the near future."

Jacques was depressed. Very depressed. Maria had caught him at just the wrong time. And her jollity had exacerbated his depression.

A moment later, Jacques heard footsteps running down the hallway.

"Oh, oh, trouble." One did not normally run inside of the Consulate offices.

And then the Consul General, Dick Williams, Maria's father, burst into Jacques' office, saying, "No. No. It was a joke. We made up the letter. You're not fired."

Dick was ready to put his arms around Jacques, anything to relieve him of the obvious distress on his face, perhaps on both faces. The Consul General told Jacques that Maria had come back to the apartment bouncing in to announce, "It worked. It worked. I think he is going to cry."

The Consul General, bless his soul, said, "Listening to Maria's description I thought that you were going to throw yourself off the building (on the eleventh floor). That's why I ran."

There are lots of ways to keep up morale in a small post.

Paragraphs

Don't go to the market in Guangzhou. He did. No electricity. No refrigeration. Fresh vegetables. Fresh meat. Killed before your eyes. You know it is fresh. Scaly pangolins with their scales ripped off before your eyes. You know it is fresh. Don't go to the market in Guangzhou.

***

The Pike Place Market. In Seattle. Everyone goes there. But you can't get it there. You have to go to the market in Guangzhou. Only in the winter months. "Good News" time. Wander past the fruit and the vegetables. Smell the small smoky cooking fires. Smell the … … I can't say it. On the spit. Turning slowly. See. But don't look. The roasting dog is turning. Dog chops. Rib of dog. Is it my dog?

***